Citizen Ambassadors

Guidelines for Responding to Questions Asked about America

by Charles T. Vetter, Jr.

with Foreword and Section Introductions by W. Ladd Hollist

Brigham Young University David M. Kennedy International Center

Library of Congress Cataloging in Publication Data

Vetter, Charles T.
  Citizen Ambassadors.

  1. United States—Miscellanea.   2. United States—Relations—Foreign countries.
  I. Title.
E156.V47   1983   973   83-7677
ISBN 0-912575-00-X (pbk.)

This publication is available from:
  Brigham Young University
  David M. Kennedy International Center
  Publication Services
  130 Faculty Office Building
  Provo, Utah 84602
  801 378-6528

Table of Contents

Preface

This book is for those who travel abroad (for whatever reasons) or who host international visitors in the United States. Because whether in their own backyards or as they travel within the United States, non-U.S. residents have many questions about America. At the casual level these questions tend to be non-controversial, but when given the opportunity, these questions can become penetrating, if not outright hostile.

Even the latter type of questions should be expected, however. No nation can perform the role played by the United States for so many years without evoking concerns and questions from people around the world. Even given the changing American role in an increasingly interdependent world, the past, present, and future of America in the world will be a topic of legitimate concern to everyone in the world.

Many Americans intuitively respond rather well even to the more belligerent types of questions. But others often respond in such a way as to foster ill-will and anti-American feelings. And more often than not, it is not the *substance* of the response but rather the *style* or *manner* of the response which brings adverse results. This volume is a collection of some of the most frequently asked questions about the United States and a *way* or *style* of responding to those questions.

As will be seen throughout this volume, the style is non-confrontational. It is a style through which answers are fashioned carefully as to avoid frontal assaults against the implied tone and often critical context of the questions. This style purposefully avoids defensive responses which, more often than not, generate more "heat," but less "light." On the other hand, this style does not encourage waffling or avoiding the critical heart of the question. You can best understand this approach by reading some or all of the questions and answers which follow and then by turning to the epilogue of this volume in which some useful guidelines for interpersonal exchanges with those from other countries are summarized.

It is also important for the reader to understand that the answers to the questions contained in this book are not meant to be definitive. The reader may feel more comfortable developing substantially different responses than those which follow. The answers contained in this book are "good," however, because they demonstrate very effectively and efficiently the non-confrontational style described above. On a personal note, as I read the following questions and answers, I noted that I would have developed quite different responses for a number of questions. But I found myself developing my different responses following the non-confrontational style illustrated herein. As a result of that, my responses were much better than they otherwise would have been.

In an attempt to help understand the changing global context which gives rise to the types of questions contained in thes book, Dr. W. Ladd Hollist has written a foreword and section introductions for this volume. Dr. Hollist is a Professor of Political Science and an Associate of the Center for International and Area Studies at Brigham Young University. He received his Ph.D. at the University of Denver and most recently taught at the University of Southern California before joining the Department of Political Science at Brigham Young University. His specialties are Latin American affairs and international political economy, and he has traveled and lived abroad extensively.

The following questions, answers, and, more importantly, the response style are the contributions of Dr. Charles T. Vetter, Jr., who, for over thirty years, has worked as a senior training officer for the foreign service. He has also been a skilled consultant and popular lecturer to literally thousands of private and governmental organizations. During his world spanning career, he has collected, tested, and learned to respond readily, openly, and comfortably to typical questions asked of Americans.

But Dr. Vetter is the last to suggest that his answers are the only appropriate responses. He and the publishers are committed to the *style* of his responses, not to their content. Hence, this is not a handbook from which answers to questions may be drawn but rather an attempt to illustrate a very important and frequently overlooked *way* of responding to such questions.

A separate acknowledgement is also due Mr. V. Lynn Tyler, Coordinator of Research and Resource Services at the Center for International and Area Studies, and his assistant Veronique Longmire, without whose insight and persistence this project would never have been conceived nor carried out. A special thank you is also due Deborah L. Coon, Manager of Publication Services at the Center for International and Area Studies. And, for varying degrees of editorial and secretarial assistance, We wish to thank Pamela Jackson, Michelle Moulton, Connie Westover, Jeri Pace, Paul Taylor, Donna Parkinson, Glen Cannon, David Hatch, and Anita Moon.

Finally, we at the Center for International and Area Studies at Brigham Young University wish to sincerely thank Dr. Vetter for allowing us to edit and publish these materials. It is our hope that by publishing them, more Americans will be able to communicate and interact more amicably and productively with citizens of other nations. We raise this hope in the full realization that our world is today more intertwined than during any previous period of history. Sophisticated transportation and communication systems have bridged what in earlier times were "natural or geographic barriers" to cross-national and cross-cultural interchange. At the same time, political, social, economic, and cultural barriers too often persist, though not insurmountably.

Our citizens deal more directly (without governments as intermediaries) and more frequently with citizens of other nations than was even thought possible a few years ago. Witness the unexpected increase in communication, travel, and diverse interchange with even such lands as China and the Soviet Union. If this volume can in even a slight way make those interchanges less traumatic, more productive, or less conflicting, then this modest publication will have served its intended purpose.

Stan A. Taylor, Director
Center for International and Area Studies
Brigham Young University

Introduction

Books and articles proclaim the 1980s and 1990s the "Information Era," the "Age of Interdependence," and the "Global Village." In this kind of environment, Americans will increasingly be representing our country as citizen ambassadors.

An important aspect of international dialogue and communication is the ability to respond to the questions, criticisms, and feelings of other peoples. Because of the impact of American society on their lives, people in other nations have many questions and concerns about the United States. They want information and answers that will help them better interact and live with Americans. They want understanding of various aspects of American life, ranging from society and culture to economics and foreign policy. In my experience, too often Americans are not able to communicate the information needed to increase understanding of their country. This book offers well-tested information that can promote that understanding in critical areas of concern to other peoples.

There are few "answers" in this book. This is not material for apologetics or debate. Rather, these responses illustrate the attitudes and approaches that I have found helpful and effective through my years of experience in dealing with foreigners in *conversational* situations. I, myself, vary my approach or selection of information in different countries or with different kinds of people. I hope to give readers examples and context that will help focus their own experiences and information in order to become more articulate in explaining our country to others.

Through my experiences as a teacher, foreign service officer, training officer, and counselor, I have come to believe that in representing America, officially or otherwise, attitudes are often more important than information. I have seen too many well-informed Americans damage international relationships with their arrogance, apathy, or intolerance. I have also seen Americans with limited information or international experience do remarkable jobs as international communicators and represesntatives because of their sincere interest, desire to share, caring for others' concerns, and recognition of the importance of understanding between cultures. Of course, the most effective people are those who are both well-informed and well-motivated.

This book will be useful for Americans both in foreign countries and those entertaining foreign visitors in the United States. Perhaps even foreign visitors themselves will find this volume to be helpful. I have also found this material useful in political and social science classes in American schools where it offers an added perspective and motivation in studying American history and institutions.

I hope this book will help the readers, whoever they might be, in making a contribution to the effective exchange of ideas, goods, services, and goodwill between the United States and its neighbors throughout the world. Such contributions can make a peaceful and productive international community possible.

This book is dedicated to the hundreds of national employees of American missions and organizations in countries around the world who have shared their experiences, insights and feelings with me about the preparation of Americans coming to work with them in their countries.

Special gratitude goes to my colleagues on the national staffs of the United States Information Service posts in over 100 countries who have served their people and our people so faithfully on the bridge between their cultures and our culture, their national interests and our national interests, their governments and our government. Their friendship and insights have been an inspiration in my training career.

Charles T. Vetter, Jr.

Foreword

Interpersonal Communications in an Interdependent World

In many respects, ours is a "new" world. The rules and regulations of international commerce, diplomacy, and travel have experienced profound shocks requiring significant adjustments. In a world markedly less easily dominated by American power and influence, we are finding that once well-proven actions and behaviors are increasingly counter- productive. The time-tested mores and practices of well-experienced, internationally involved citizens of the United States have indeed been called into question. Our world is more interdependent; we are more vulnerable, while others are less vulnerable, to changes and behaviors that occur in international affairs.

In 1973, Henry Kissinger, then Secretary of State, characterized this "new," more interdependent world: "[Although militarily] there are two superpowers, [economically] there are at least five major groupings. Power is no longer homogeneous." He went on to assert that throughout history, "military, economic, and political power were closely related. To be powerful, a nation had to be strong in all categories." Claiming this was no longer so, Kissinger concluded, ". . . military muscle does not guarantee political influence. Economic giants can be militarily weak, and military strength may not be able to obscure economic weakness." (Kissinger, October 10, 1973, News Release, Bureau of Public Affairs, Department of State.)

Relatively speaking, our world was less complex when we knew more confidently what our status was in the world and what our position was on a wide spectrum of issues. While the burdens of world leadership surely did not pass us by—witness the challenges of Berlin, Korea, and Vietnam to name a few—we at least could be relatively certain that our country was in the "driver's seat," steering the course of world affairs. It was not entirely incorrect to presume that whether it be in political, military, economic, or social spheres, ours was the leadership role. Moreover, we could generally act upon the premise that all of these concerns were linked together and that we could exact compliance in one sphere by rewarding or punishing nations in that sphere or in related spheres. For example, it seemed fairly reasonable to suspect that for our provision of security from the threats of communism, nations of the free world should and would be willing to "pay" us through support of U.S. positions in other areas.

Clearly these expectations of "issue linkage," that agreement in one sphere necessarily suggests a willingness or even obligation for agreement in other spheres, are far from realistic today. The agenda of global issues is more fragmented than it has been in the recent past. Being opposed to Soviet or U.S. intervention in the internal affairs of a nation does not necessarily mean that the affected nation wishes to increase its alliance with the nonintervening nation. Nor can we suppose that because nations agree with us on a particular trade issue, for example, that they will similarly agree with us on non- trade related issues that affect us both. Agreement or support among nations is not wrapped in one solid, indivisible package now. Agreements are far more related to specific issues than has been the case.

Some of this softening of once fairly stable international alliances, a softening born of a willingness of nations to collaborate on some issues while strongly conflicting on others, makes international affairs less predictable and imminently more complex. And, as some might assert, the prospects of violent conflicts are surely increased by this "new" context for world affairs.

Yet, in this less coherent world we have not necessarily lessened the frequency or intensity of our involvements in other countries. Our industrial and agro-business corporations are as active, if not more active, as direct investors in the countries of the world as during any period of their history. Moreover, our major banking institutions have dramatically increased their presence in numerous nations. Our outreach in the name of national security has certainly not decreased. Such transnational dealings may have even contributed to the aforementioned separation of political, military, and economic issues in the world.

Nor have we as yet abdicated the role we have played for so long, that of a world leader. In fact, we seem intent on promoting our leadership role. Yet, we do so in a world which we no longer dominate; we attempt leadership in a complex, interdependent world that is much different from that in which we learned our "leadership skills." So different that the very definition of "leadership" is now unclear.

These several developments have produced numerous uncertainties. From out of a period of relative stability has emerged a period of flux and confusion. So pervasive has been this uncertainty that a new industry has been born to cope with it. The business of political risk analysis—the trade of assessing the likelihood of political, economic, and social changes within specific cultures, countries, or across the globe—is flourishing. But even such analyses come with little expectation that the forecasts will be born out within any acceptable degree of accuracy. It may well be the case that the most honest and accurate characterization of our plight is simply that we do not know what the future will bring—either in specific geographic areas or relative to certain issues.

Historically, during periods of flux and transition such as ours, nations have pursued different courses. Some have sought to recapture the grandeur and dominance they once enjoyed. Former world powers have gone to great lengths to resist their decline. They have turned to military combat, strong economic policies, or vigorous promotion of their cultural traditions in an attempt to regain at least a portion of the powerful role they once enjoyed.

It seems that we, as a nation, or we as our nation's diplomats, international merchants, business executives, or other frequent international travelers, have but two choices to make during this period of increasing global interdependence. First, we, like those from formerly powerful nations before us, can vigorously defend and uphold the virtues and might of the United States. Such strong national feelings amidst our interdependent world environment will likely reap undesired outcomes, conflict, and even violence. We can urge acceptance of our traditions—political, economic, cultural and social—by the nations of the world. More

3

likely than not, such urgings will be ill-received; many nations, in the guise of their own nationalism, will denounce such actions as blatant interventions in their internal affairs. In a similar fashion, we can simply assert our "rights" to world resources that we have for long periods of time consumed in proportions far in excess of our share of the world's population. We could claim that these resources are ours by right of historical usage and by our ability to pay the highest price of all competing buyers and consumers. Again, such claims now more than ever before will be inflammatory. Making such claims, or otherwise blatantly defending what we may perceive to be in the best interests of the United States, will likely damage interpersonal and international activities with those of other nations and cultures.

The second option is to somehow willingly cooperate with other nations without always trying to steer the actions of those nations in directions that are consistent with a narrow, nationalistic definition of our interests. While potentially less likely to incite opposition from those with whom we interact internationally, this option seems to some to guarantee the complete and final decline of the United States. To them it seems to connote too much loss of power and influence. Still, if ours is indeed an interdependent world, if we can no longer impose our national interest position on such a world, cooperation and collaboration seems to be a prudent course. In such collaboration we need not compromise our proper principles of economic efficiency, political security, and fair dealings. Rather, in lessening international conflict and resentment, we might more surely obtain goals consistent with such principles.

Arguing that the world system has changed, that it has become more interdependent, and that we must adapt to such changes by altering our strategies and tactics of world leadership, is not to suggest that any kind of success will be easily realized. Realism demands recognition of deepseated ideological and cultural chasms that divide the nations of the world. Surely these will not be easily bridged; perhaps the best we can do is to highlight the catastrophic costs of not bridging such chasms that block the path of world integration.

We are suggesting, however, that disagreements among one time allies and vigorous demands from formerly subservient nations are on the increase. Will we try to curb such disagreements and demands with the tools of power politics? Will we use threats to arrest the emergence of dissent in the world community? Or will we recognize that such changes require changed political and economic practices?

Surely there will be times when the interests of the United States cannot be served except by energetic and even forceful actions. History virtually guarantees that such is the lot of any major power. At the same time, it is perhaps possible that our interests are increasingly global in scope; that even our personal lives are dependent upon global activities. Even the dynamics of our national productivity and job formation are obviously impacted by international developments. And while we cannot single-handedly steer those global dynamics to create our own "preferred world," we likely will achieve more of our goals via cooperation and collaboration than via conflict.

But there is one thing we can "single-handedly" accomplish. As increasing global interdependence results in more and more Americans dealing with people from other nations, and as America's changing world status occasions more and more questions from abroad about U.S. actions and policies, we can all learn to be more sensitive in dealing with these questions. The linkage between individual actions and international affairs is very complex and indirect, at best. But there is such a linkage. The changing international environment just described does not lessen the obligation we all have to communicate more effectively across cultures. Rather, it increases this need.

Dr. W. Ladd Hollist
Professor of Political Science
Brigham Young University

List of Questions
Frequently Asked Americans

SECTION I: AMERICAN CULTURE AND SOCIETY

1. Describe American family life for us. Is it true that the wife runs the husband and the children run the mother?

2. Isn't most of your divorce, juvenile delinquency, and unemployment caused by your women working outside the home?

3. Since American women have supermarkets and myriads of modern machines, what do they do with all their extra time? Why women's liberation? Liberation from what? Aren't a lot of these women working outside their homes because they find home life dull and without challenge?

4. Why do you put your old people in homes for the aged? Isn't this an example of your family life being destroyed?

5. Consider your American divorce rate. Is this breakdown of the family brought on by a system that inevitably produces an inferior quality of life, even though you have so many resources and fine people?

6. Tell me, isn't American society too free, too permissive? Doesn't this American dating practice, where your young people go out without any chaperons, lead to promiscuity, to easy sex? Isn't this one reason why you have so many illegitimate births among your young ladies, particularly your teenagers? Aren't you becoming an immoral society?

7. Are Americans really happy? If they are, why do so many need psychiatrists and drugs? Why your violence and cults?

8. Why is there so much crime and violence in the United States when you are supposed to be such a law-abiding people? Is it safe to go anywhere? Won't I get mugged, or attacked, or robbed?

9. You blame our people for producing and supplying narcotics, marijuana, and such things to your country. But, if you didn't have so many psychologically disturbed people, so many drug addicts in the United States that create a market, we would not have a huge international drug problem. What is wrong with your society?

10. Why do white people in America hate black people, Mexicans, and other minorities?

11. Why are your Indians so bad off? Are they still being forced to live on reservations, and aren't they deprived of their rights and opportunities?

12. Do you think another Catholic (like Kennedy) could be elected President? Aren't most of your people anti-Catholic?

13. Are you Americans really informed? Many of your cities have only one newspaper and the owner also owns the T.V. or radio stations. Most of your news in America comes from very superficial television. It is so superficial you may get no real news at all. You can go months without seeing anything about important countries like Germany, Japan, Nigeria, Brazil, Turkey or India.

14. Why don't people from the United States living in our country mix with our people? You live in "capitalistic ghettos" and do not bother to learn our customs and our language.

15. Why do your people know so little about us and our country? You know nothing about our people, our cities, our politics, our govern-

8

ment. Doesn't this really prove that Americans are not interested in anybody else, especially our country?

16. I'm quite interested in sending my child to America to study, but many people say that your schools neglect the fundamentals; they neglect the discipline and the culture, things that are so important. Your modern facilities are beautiful, but your people don't use them; the students never take advantage of these things. I think that the British school system is much better, don't you also think so?

17. Why is it that Americans do not have strong philosophies and spiritual convictions? I expect that it is because you are such pragmatic, materialistic people. You do not have the spirit and the soul for philosophy or for conceptualizing profound ideas and principles.

18. Why do you send such bad movies and television programs to our country which corrupt our youth and also hurt the American reputation?

19. Aren't you Americans really weak because you are getting almost everything you need without really working for it? You think this jogging, this ridiculous jogging, people running around for no purpose, is going to really help you? Why not put your energies into more meaningful purposes?

SECTION II: AMERICAN GOVERNMENT

20. In watching your 1980 elections, I did not really see the difference between your Democratic Party and Republican Party. What is the difference? Where did Anderson fit in?

21. How can a peanut farmer and a movie actor even try to get the presidency? What were their qualifications? We should have experienced people in positions with as much power in the world as the American president has. How do these people get elected?

22. Who makes policy in the United States now? Presidents Johnson, Nixon, Ford and Carter made agreements and your congress turned them down. And now it is doing the same thing to President Reagan. How can we negotiate with you? How can we depend on you?

23. Isn't it true that American businesses, the monopolies, the multinational corporations, are really the ones that determine American foreign policy in your country? Aren't the military industrialists and the sci-

entists the ones that really are controlling American foreign policy around the world?

24. How can you let public servants strike—your teachers, farmers, truck drivers, and police? Strikes can create chaos in America. How can you have control if everybody is doing their own thing?

25. With your Freedom of Information Act, and irresponsible officials and journalists—who often reveal government secrets—how can you have good security for diplomacy and intelligence? Isn't the CIA useless now?

26. Is it true that millions of people cannot afford medical care in your country? Why can't you have a government program where everybody can get health care with dignity?

27. When you have a democratic constitution, why do your people have to fight for civil rights? If you're really a democracy, people should have their civil rights.

28. Is your law humane when you still have capital punishment?

29. You Americans say you are against socialism. What is so wrong with socialism? We cannot afford your wasteful ways. We just do not have the resources.

30. In Europe, we have quite a bit of difficulty in collecting taxes. How do you get people to pay?

31. Wasn't President Kennedy's assassination part of a conspiracy of your far right (or far left), both to remove your progressive president and to increase international tension? Isn't Ted Kennedy in danger today?

SECTION III: AMERICANS IN THE WORLD ECONOMY

32. Why doesn't the United States support the Third World and its efforts for a New Economic Order?

33. Why do you let your businessmen get rich on our country's wealth by exploiting our natural resources and then selling over-priced American goods to us? And why do you claim that you are helping our people when your aid only makes the rich richer and does not help our poor people?

34. The decisions of multinational corporations affect the lives of millions, yet who knows how they are operated? Who really runs ITT?

Are the multinationals neo-imperialist organizations fronting for U.S. business interests?

35. Why is it that U.S. aid programs such as those in Latin America and Africa do not work? Are these just ploys to make us dependent on the Yankees?

36. Americans have been in our country for so long; you make promises and expect us to follow your directions. Do you think you can buy our friendship with these assistance programs?

37. Many of us believe that capitalism is inhumane. Isn't socialism much more "Christian" than capitalism, much more humane, much more promoting of the welfare and love and friendship among people in different classes, among different kinds of people? Your capitalism is inhumane. Just look at what is happening in your country: the crime, the violence, and the racism.

38. Isn't your use of energy, your use of oversized cars and endless appliances both selfish and irresponsible? If the world oil supply falls short, those of us in smaller countries will suffer. You have the power to get what you need. Besides, your demands have driven prices up, causing inflation and endangering our economy.

39. Why is there an American energy crisis? Doesn't this indicate bad planning and waste, and perhaps dishonesty in your big oil companies?

40. How can you have poverty and unemployment in your country when you are so rich? How can you have poverty in the midst of so much skill, science, technology, resources, and education?

SECTION IV: AMERICAN FOREIGN POLICY

41. Does the United States really want disarmament? What would your monopolists and military men do if you really disarmed?

42. Are you really sincere about détente? Why do you spend so much money on arms and sell so many arms to other people, even to our country? Why do you export all these arms? Do you really want peace? Do you really want détente? Hasn't Reagan gone back to the Cold War?

43. Why are your leaders arguing over the SALT Treaties and nuclear freezes? Your NATO allies have agreed with the SALT Treaty, and yet you don't sign it yourself. Don't you want to stop the arms race?

44. Why is the Soviet Union surpassing America in science and military power? Is it because their education system and their discipline are better than yours?

45. Third World insecurity is growing as America seems to get weaker. We have relied on you in the past and yet you seem to be losing power. Is your power shrinking?

46. Why did the governments of Iran and Vietnam collapse? Didn't you desert them? Didn't you abandon your friends in Taiwan? Will you let other allies down? How do we look at American power today?

47. Explain American actions in Vietnam, Cambodia, and Laos. Didn't you defy international law and human decency by bombing North Vietnam? Why did you intervene in a civil war in South Vietnam? Wasn't this North American neo-colonialism? Wasn't your policy wrong? It even ruined your own economy.

48. Are you Americans still trying to police the world even after what happened in Vietnam? Look at what you are doing in the Persian Gulf. What are you Americans doing with your power?

49. Wasn't your intervention in Chile, Israel and Iran a return to your "big stick" policies of the 1920's and before? If we have a revolution you do not approve of in our country, will you intervene again?

50. Do your people really support the policy of intervening in the domestic affairs of Latin American republics that your leaders consider communistic or in violation of your ideas of human rights? Don't you think that AID restrictions imposed by your congress were an insult to these countries?

51. Why do you insist on our being anti-communist? Why can't you let us be friends with everyone? Why do you discourage our trade with communist countries? Isn't this just "superpower" politics?

52. Why do you send us such inept ambassadors and other representatives who try to intervene in our country? Why do so many not know anything about our people and not speak our language?

53. Why don't you give all of the Panama Canal back to Panama now?

54. What is the Peace Corps? Are they really CIA agents, or are they just young people who can't get jobs?

55. Why has the United States been picking on some of its friends over the human rights issue? Don't you realize that strong measures are needed to protect society against attacks by terrorist groups? Look at how you sabotaged your friends in Iran.

56. Many people say your position on human rights is hypocritical since you still discriminate against blacks and other minorities. How do you justify passing judgment on other countries?

57. How can the U.S. explain the inconsistency of its policy in denying arms credit to Uruguay and Argentina because of human rights violations while making vast shipments of arms to the Middle East, Korea, and elsewhere?

58. Will this Egyptian-Israeli Treaty work? In helping to set it up, didn't you abandon other allies in the Middle East, like the Saudis? They opposed this treaty. Also, you are not adequately considering the Palestinians.

59. Why have you pressured and isolated Cuba? They could not hurt you! You have even reconciled with China.

60. You are supposed to be leaders of the democratic world. Why do you support dictatorships and military juntas?

Responses to Questions Asked about America

Section I:
American Culture and Society

When so many societies have come to look upon the United States as an example of so many strengths and virtues, it is not surprising that now many are chagrined over our rapid cultural change and perhaps even moral decay. For many, our nobility is now tarnished as we are experiencing a break down of the family unit, increases in crimes of violence, drug abuse, and social decline. Others take offense at our seeming narrowness when we interact with them in their own countries.

And, when there is little question that we are experiencing nothing short of a cultural revolution in so many aspects of American life, we will appear hollow if we frontally deny what are often quite sound perceptions. Dr. Vetter's answers to the questions regarding American culture and society illustrate some general concepts that we would all do well to communicate to those persons making similar inquiries of us.

First, we would do well to recognize that American society is in flux.

We are experiencing a massive sociological and cultural transformation. During this period of rapid change—technological, social, and cultural— we have come upon undesirable developments not anticipated when we embarked on what appeared to be a glorious road to economic and political progress. Our rapid industrialization with increasingly rapid technological innovation has dramatically altered our patterns of living. As yet we have not been able to make appropriate social and cultural adaptations. The norms or pillars of psychological and community security that the family unit, agrarian communities, and neighborhood churches once provided in our pre-industrial order have often been called into question in our quicker-paced, urban, highly mobile and widely traveled, contemporary society. While we might fervently wish for a return to those mores and norms, and while that may be the eventual decision of our society, it is nonetheless the case that we are in the midst of a significant period of transition. Transition brings uncertainty, and nowhere is this more evident than in the challenges now confronting our social and cultural institutions.

We would do well to point to the seeming inevitability of such social and cultural transformation that awaits countries just now embarking on significant industrialization, urbanization, and overall "modernization." These are not issues that will only confront our society. These are issues which have been or soon will be confronted by many nations in the world. Recognition of this rapid cultural and social change, plus the assertion that such transformation is not the sole burden of the United States, are elements often found in Dr. Vetter's response to questions.

Second, those behaviors that are questionable but widely evident to almost any observer are not without opposition in America. For instance, many are boldly facing up to the social and cultural problems we are now confronting. We seem willing to face up to the problem of declining quality in our public schools. While not yet having general solutions, at least we have progressed to the point of recognizing the problems. Crimes of violence are not met only with quiet resignation and apathy. We may now be to the point where we are ready to address the problem. Substance abuse, including the usage of drugs of all sorts, has finally provoked some resolute foes into action. And, quite interestingly, some of the strongest foes of drug abuse are those that at one time or another were users themselves.

The point to be made is that while we are not without our social and cultural problems, neither are we without persons willing to engage their energies in seeking solutions. Moreover, in the recognition that many of these social and cultural problems are not solely our own, we invite others to join with us. While there are those that persist in their attitude of complacency or even outright delight with what to others are morally and culturally corrupt practices, we are not without sincere efforts to solve these problems. Again, this is a theme often invoked in Dr. Vetter's answers to questions often raised about American culture and society.

Dr. Vetter addresses questions concerning the evident transformation of the American family. He gives balanced answers to querries as to whether women's liberation is at the root of these changes in the family. He addresses the changed relationships among the parents and children of many families. He focuses on the social origins of our drug abuse problems and increases in crime. In so doing he does not deny our social problems, but rather tries to explain how they have come about and what may be required if we are to satisfactorily adapt to these changes. And, finally, Dr. Vetter assesses why Americans tend to be uninvolved with the segments of foreign societies which they visit. He offers an interesting assessment of the seeming narrowness of American citizens that go abroad.

And, while each of these are important points unto themselves, we would do well to recognize the general approach taken in answering the questions. The approach is purposely non-defensive; no attempt is made to duck the question by claiming that still, on balance, the American society and culture is superior to any other. Rather, the attempt is made to engage the questioner in the need to find answers to the social and cultural disruptions so often associated with these types of questions. It is as important to catch the tone of the answers given as it is to have a pat answer to specific questions that one is likely to face.

QUESTION 1

Describe American family life for us. Is it true that the wife runs the husband and the children run the mother?
RESPONSE

This is a frequent line of inquiry about kinds of things that I would discuss in connection with the American family. Many are the consequences of urbanization and mobility (at least one American family in five changes its place of residence each year). It means that much of the "compadre" system or the extended family system, so common in other parts of the world, has changed. In the United States the tendency is more common for a nuclear family (children and the parents) to live separately from grandparents, uncles and aunts.

19

It certainly seems to many people that the woman is running the husband in pushing for "woman's rights," especially by going out of the home into the work force. What has happened is that instead of having a man-dominated family as we had in the early days of our republic, or perhaps the second stage where the man was the senior partner and the woman the junior partner, now, particularly with increasing two-income families, couples have to work together as a team, more as equals. They negotiate family functions. Because of these trends toward equality, it sometimes seems like the woman runs the family. However, I have seen more female dictators in extended family societies where the oldest woman in a large family has dictatorial power over the younger women and often the younger men. I have seen it in Japan, India, and South America.

Our children, in this permissive, youth-oriented, youth-dominated age, have seemed undisciplined to other people. They seem to often dominate their parents. There is some truth to this. In families that have broken up, working parents often develop a guilt complex and tend to be overindulgent and overcompensating. But in the final analysis, you will find that children do not "run" their parents, although there is certainly a whole different structure of relationships in the U.S. today than when I was young.

When people have alternatives, it is much harder to be a dictator. It is much harder for a man to control a woman when she has alternatives, and it is much harder for parents to control children when children are getting much of their influence from television, from their peers, and from their schools. They are spending less time in the collective assembly of family discipline or family living situations.

QUESTION 2

Isn't most of your divorce, juvenile delinquency, and unemployment caused by your women working outside the home?
RESPONSE

There is a lot said about the Latin-American Tradition of "machismo," which gives the authoritative role to men. The woman's role is usually defined as that of taking care of the home and the children. The increasing educational level, mobility, participation of women, economic resources, opportunities for jobs and careers has changed the nature of the American family. It is also changing some of the roles and functions of the husband and wife in the home. I know in our marriage I wash a lot of dishes. As a matter of fact, my wife is now working as an executive director of an organization, and I am now working with my office in our

20

home. I am home cleaning up the dog dirt and putting out the trash, and all of the things that she did for so many years in supporting my career. I am even doing a lot of the chauffeuring to get her to meetings that she has to attend. In a sense, in millions of families, there has been a redefinition of many aspects of marriage in recent years. This is particularly true with young people where economic demands and their preference for a certain standard of living have made it necessary for the wife to work outside of the home.

Now, I think that in any analysis of changing family patterns you can trace much of the family disintegration to three or four elements, part of which are attributable to the woman going out of the home. One is that the wife comes home and does not have enough time with the children, does not discipline them enough and they tend to drift more toward the influence of their peers and people outside the home, especially at school and in watching so much television. This has had a major effect within the family, where the quality of the time they spend together has been recognized as a very real problem. This problem is developing in most countries where television viewing eats up hours of the day.

The television problem is quite separate from the woman being outside of the home, though it does further limit the time she spends with her husband and children. Again, the woman going out of the home is a result of a changing society. I have talked to older people who talk about the "olden days." I see some of the wide-spread misery of the past generation, in contrast to the advantages in life that usually came only to the rich or to the people who had servants. As a matter of fact, all through English history, including the Churchill family history, the upperclass English would delegate the raising of their children to servants or nannies. They would send them off to private schools. Yet the English are supposed to be great family people. It is just that we are in a period of transition. There are trade-offs, casualities and costs that you have to recognize when there is such a vast social revolution going on.

To say that divorce and juvenile delinquency happen just because women are working outside of the home may be faulty. I can show you many cases where a family's standard of living and education are increased because the woman is working and making an income. This makes education, mobility, good health, and good living conditions possible because she provides additional income and is organized well enough to be a "superwoman," as the saying goes. She may still be a good mother, take care of her husband, be a good hostess, a good worker in her office, etc. This is a very challenging problem, but it is part of the changing patterns that are taking place with industrialization, modernization, and urbanization all over the world. It is certainly impacting very heavily on the United States society. All nations would be well advised to examine remedies and constructive alternatives.

QUESTION 3

Since American women have supermarkets and myriads of modern machines, what do they do with all the extra time? Why women's liberation? Liberation from what? Aren't a lot of these women working outside their homes because they find home life dull and without challenge?

RESPONSE

This is a fascinating area for discussion, although it is very hard to generalize for a population the size of the U.S. I know the women's liberation movement has gathered great force in the U.S. In the early history of the North American continent, with immigration from rather urbanized European countries to the original thirteen colonies of the United States, there was no servant-class. Women had to share in the work, risk, and education in a way that was generally not the case in Europe, or even in the Asian or African cultures from which they or their ancestors had come.

There has been a change in family relationships. I have heard sociologists talk about the original family pattern much like that of Europe, Asia, or Africa where the man was dominant and the woman had the responsibility of feeding and caring for the children in the home. The power and the authority in the family belonged to the man. This continued for some two centuries until the Victorian period allowed women more strength and authority. Thereafter, women often developed resources of their own, allowing them a greater range of choices. But the man, until relatively recently, was the dominant person or senior partner.

In recent times more marriages have evolved into a partnership pattern when both the man and the woman are employed. The women often work to obtain the additional finances necessary to attain the standard of living that they desire. Often this has created problems in family life. About 42% of the American work force presently consists of women. In such a situation more equality in employment practices and pay scales is necessary.

Furthermore, the tremendous development of technology, including home labor-saving equipment, has increased the physical productivity of men and women. Thus the time involved in doing the family chores has been drastically reduced. In a sense this has "liberated" women from the

22

drudgery of the past centuries for other things such as using their minds, talents and creativity in other fields. This may be one of the main reasons why upper middle-class women have gone to work. A lightened work load opens new vistas. The weight of extra time induces boredom at home for many.

With urbanization, there has been a breakup of extended family networks. One no longer has uncles, aunts, grandmothers, and grandfathers playing an intimate role in the family. The social interaction of "meeting around the well," and other community activities of women while the men are off working have virtually disappeared. The communal places that have traditionally kept women occupied and interacting are vanishing. They feel that they want to be with more people as well as to be productive and creative. I think that these have been some of the sociological and psychological factors that have brought more women into the work force outside the home.

When women get an education and mobility, they feel that they have a right to participate in those things that affect their lives, feelings, and productivity. Women's liberation, as perceived by its proponents, is something that sees women as human beings, irrespective of sex, demanding fair and equitable participation and treatment in life.

QUESTION 4

Why do you put your old people in homes for the aged? Isn't this an example of your family life being destroyed?

RESPONSE

The question about America and its old people is something that comes up many times. In the past, children were the social security of old people. This is still true in most parts of the world.

In the U.S., I think we have developed more independence between generations. More and more parents have decided that they do not want to be a burden on their children. Also, a social welfare program began with social security programs, pensions, government payments, and retirement schemes that reduced the older people's dependence on the young.

When my grandmother was forty or forty-five, she was an old woman, relying on her children. Americans are now living to be 70 or 75 and they are not about to take orders from someone many years younger, who, in their eyes, is still a kid. They want to be independent, they want to live their own lives, and they do not want to be a burden on their children. Gray power is a manifestation of the increasing number of old people who want to live independently. Twenty-seven million people in the United States are over the age of 65. This will increase to around 35 million within 10 years. Only 5% of the people over 65 years are in nursing or retirement homes. The rest are living independently or with family members.

So, there has been a change in family care. Today, it is common for children to move away from their parents and grandparents. And we have a new phenomena of people living so long that once a husband and wife get their children through school and into their own lives, they then have to take care of their aged parents. To simplify things, there is a whole new development to take care of older people in retirement villages and retirement homes. This is becoming one of the fast developing new service industries.

Japan seems to just now be encountering these changes. For years, the old have been venerated and the families have taken care of them. Today, however, the Japanese are living beyond the age of 45 or 50 years, the average life expectancy in the 1940's. Since they are living even longer, the country is having problems with pensions and with old people needing care and assistance. Some older people are often outliving their families.

This is a problem that is coming to all industrialized, modernized societies that have a lengthened life span. They suddenly must cope with a larger number of elderly citizens who are living past the age of productivity into the age of senescence. One solution to this modern problem is building communities and homes for the aged.

In our society, women live much longer than their husbands, (an average of 10 years, but often 20 to 25 years). If they do not have families, there must be some private or public facility to take care of these elderly citizens.

The great majority are living on their own resources, alone, or with their families, but there is an increasing number that need help. Some families find that in the very advanced stages of debility or sickness, a nursing home or old persons' home is the wise solution for proper care, particulary if all family members are working outside of the home. The nursing home or old persons' home industry has grown to provide a service for many people who find it desirable for their personal lives and for the lifestyle of their families.

And while sadness and concern for the elderly still exists, a large portion of the aged segment of our population is living fruitfully and productively. Many are even going to college in their seventies. And, now that we have raised the compulsory retirement age, we find more productive, self-sustaining people who in former generations would have been dead at their age.

24

QUESTION 5

Consider your American divorce rate. Is this breakdown of the family brought on by a system that inevitably produces an inferior quality of life, even though you have so many resources and fine people?

RESPONSE

Science, education, and work have improved the quality and length of life of the masses in much of the world. But that very progress and change has brought new problems, like overpopulation and divorce. Divorce is a tremendous tragedy that reflects the impact of change on most societies today. I myself have gone through the divorce procedure. It was a horrible thing for me, my wife, and the children. (Happily, we eventually remarried.)

When my mother was young there was practically no divorce in America. There were few laws that made divorce even possible in many states. It was a male dominated society where a single woman had very little opportunity or alternative to married life if she left the original marriage. Also, the churches were against divorce and were a tremendous social power.

In 1975, for the first time, we had over a million divorces in the USA—a million divorces! That is two people for each divorce, plus millions of children. Divorce has a great social impact.

But I have also noticed around the world that as people really get alternatives (for example, social mobility and education), and especially as women get alternatives outside of the home for work and education, unfair and exploitive marriages are less and less possible. This is because people in a marriage today often do not have to put up with brutality, neglect, stupidity, and drunkenness as they might have when they had no other alternatives.

In the United States, as divorce laws were passed and women sought education, mobility, and opportunities, new alternatives were discovered. Men and women began to exercise these options if they were unhappy. Part of this, of course, was due to the increased mobility of the nuclear family. Generations tended to move apart. Their togetherness became superficial, maintained by telephone, and by air, train and automobile travel.

Another contrast made this possible. I remember in my father's generation, the sons usually followed their fathers into the same vocation. The great majority of jobs in my grandfather's and great-grandfather's time were rural and agricultural. So you generally followed the profession of your father or mother.

After World War I the pattern of young people was to break away, to be independent of their parents, and not be under their control and domination. They began to move to cities to get independence, liberty, and to achieve a higher standard of living. We began to see the break-up of large families. Many of the stable elements in society, many of the static elements that made family rule of old people and of parents possible, also began to evaporate as people got time and space alternatives.

I think we have seen a pattern in the United States, as well as in all industrialized countries. Urbanization is taking place even in the developing countries and divorce is increasing as people get real alternatives, and as stressful conditions increase. As a matter of fact, in the Soviet Union statistics indicate that there were nearly a million divorces during 1980 in that socialist country.

In some societies where the oldest woman in the family has had fantastic power (as occurs in Japan, India, South America) many people are revolting against "mother-in-law" power, and we are seeing divorces on the initiative of the men as well as the women.

QUESTION 6
Tell me, isn't American society too free, too permissive? Doesn't this American dating practice, where your young people go out without any chaperons, lead to promiscuity, to easy sex? Isn't this one reason why you have so many illegitimate births among your young ladies, particularly your teenagers? Aren't you becoming an immoral society?
RESPONSE
In my mother's youth this kind of dating did not occur. A young woman did not go out alone with a young man. They went out with some kind of supervision. I think the thing that disrupted this pattern was a social revolution during World War I, when women began moving and working outside of the home. People moved to different cities. Women obtained social mobility which was quite a departure from the extended family and small community life in the United States during my mother's youth in the Victorian period.

As the social custom of dating gained acceptance and popularity, words even changed in meaning. For instance, "homely" in the British English means home loving, cozy, home centered. "Homely" in American English means ugly. I think that the language change came about to describe young women who were attractive and unmarried but who were not getting dates (when dating became popular) and who were sitting home all the time. The question would increasingly come up, "Why isn't she getting any attention or dates? Why no invitations? She must not be very pretty; she must not be very datable; she must be ugly if she is in the home so much."

We have had a basic change in social patterns in the last fifty years in the United States. I do not think there is any doubt that the increasing permissiveness, the relaxation of moral rules and norms in families, communities and churches, and a lessening of accountability and discipline in family groups, have created a looseness that would certainly be considered immoral by the standards of the Victorian period or by the standards of even twenty years ago.

Of course, the question arises as to what is "immoral" in this new, pluralistic society, with its many different forms and different values? What may be immoral in one culture may be moral in another culture. What may be permissive in one culture may be accepted freedom and rational action in the context of another culture. I must say that there is a considerable amount of discussion about this on the part of our psychiatrists, welfare counselors, moralists and religious leaders.

I do think that in the United States the permissive trend has gone too far. Now we are observing a corrective trend. Many are paying more attention to family solidarity and setting standards. People realistically see the problems of non-marital and teenage sex and pregnancy outside of marriage. This is a very real problem in our society today.

I think that the best approach is to discuss a problem like this with as much personal experience and expert knowledge as you can bring to bear, remembering that the problem in the United States probably is coming very quickly to other countries in the world as societies become more complex, open, permissive, technological, and impersonalized.

We also have to recognize the change in the situation and status of women in society, and women in the family, as they have gotten more social, economic, and political mobility. Often in the past the mother and father determined the actions and set the values and the standards of young women until they were married, even until middle age.

In today's world young women have become much more autonomous, just like young men. They accept responsibility for their own behavior and actions. The dating situation now is one of mutual participation on the part of the young woman. Discretion on the woman's part is just as important as the discretion of the young man.

I should also mention that it used to be that dating was something only young people did. But now, with the number of single people who are middle-aged and even into old age (often through divorce or death of a spouse), companionship with the opposite sex has taken on quite a different connotation than it had in other times.

Are Americans really happy? If they are, why do so many need psychiatrists and drugs? Why your violence and cults?
RESPONSE

Judging from some of the surveys that have been taken recently about whether Americans would change their lives, I think in comparative terms that Americans, in general, do have a feeling of satisfaction, opportunity, hope, achievement, and a general feeling of well-being. Yet, there is much individual insecurity and unhappiness, particularly in periods of economic crisis and unemployment. In the stress of today's modernized society, in contrast to a society where large families and small communities have often been insulated against individual mental pressure, strain, and loneliness, many of the protections for the individual that existed before have vanished.

Therefore, we now find a great amount of psychological insecurity that did not exist in the past. There is more material security, but new kinds of psychological insecurity. Of the people who cannot handle these stresses, strains, and insecurities well, a large number (into the millions) will revert to some kind of compensation; they will seek relief, comfort, affiliation, or love.

Some of this is reflected in drug use. By drugs I include alcohol, narcotics, pacifiers, and tranquilizers. It is a very sad thing for many of us to see how many people have sought escape from the harshness, tension, demands, and pace of life by using drugs. Also, many people go to the extremes of anti-social behavior with criminal behavior. Beyond that, we have many who lapse into psychosis where they no longer can handle life, and they go to the radical extremes of schizophrenia and paranoia.

Many, particularly those who have the financial resources, have found professional counseling and therapy to be extremely helpful. One of the largest new professions in the United States is "counseling." It may be counseling on housing, counseling for the poor, counseling in deviant behavior, counseling for teenagers, or counseling for divorce. Here, psychological and psychiatric skills are used to help people make a realistic adjustment to the fantastic rate of change that has been taking place in every element of American society: economic, social, political, cultural, and emotional.

In this kind of an atmosphere, there are real demands for relief from the kinds of stress, strain, tension, and unhappiness that can be produced. And yet, having said all this, I think in comparative terms and reflected by many research projects that I have seen, Americans are relatively happy, proud and secure. Even though we see problems, some of which are reflected in our politics, social life, and records of violence, most people are happy, or at least not unhappy with most aspects of their lives.

Of course, many of the crimes and the cults are manifestations of these insecure times. People have reached out for affiliation, help, or release. One can trace crime to economic insecurity, unemployment, inflation, the need for money, drugs and things of this nature. And, these unhealthy signs are not just evident in the United States but all over the world, revealing that people feel that they need release, meaning, affiliation, somebody to join for help. Guidance and discipline are highly sought. This can be seen in changes in Christianity and Islam that are adjusting their practices to better help people with modern problems.

QUESTION 8

Why is there so much crime and violence in the United States when you are supposed to be such a law-abiding people? Is it safe to go anywhere? Won't I get mugged, or attacked, or robbed?
RESPONSE

I am amazed how many people visiting the United States tell me that they've been told before they leave: "Be careful, be very careful when you go to the United States. There's so much violence." Also it comes up in political criticism that Americans are violent, traditional cowboys, fighting and brawling. Of course, this is accentuated by television with its many themes of violence that are exported overseas and viewed all over the world. I think such programs heighten this violent image.

There is much violence in the United States. There is a tradition of the frontier, of physical interchange. We see it in American football, for instance, in contrast to the much more prevalent soccer/football played all over the world.

On the other hand, you have to put this into perspective. All through human history, and particularly in poorer areas, there has been a tremendous amount of violence. In earlier days in the United States there was violence, but it just was not reported as widely. People were not keeping statistics. They did not have the recording machines or the crime-apprehension mechanisms. Also there was violence in our frontier past until the instruments and institutions for keeping law and order were established.

On the other hand, this has been a violent period in history with the spread of terrorism all over the world and the frustration as people have chosen new alternatives. You no longer have the tight-knit communities where everybody knows everybody else. And then you have the added pressures of inflation and unemployment. People have the pressures to get money when they have a drug problem. People who are normally law-abiding suddenly feel the necessity to get resources, to get alcohol or money to meet new demands of society. These are some of the factors that have stimulated violent crimes. Some sociologists say violence on television, designed to capture audience attention, is also giving models of violence to the young.

On the other hand, I'm not too sure, proportionally, that there is more violent crime now. When I was young, I can remember the violent strikes and racial disorders in Detroit between different groups who would fight. They were not often recorded. There was tremendous violence with the Irish and the Poles who were always supposed to be fighting. And there was the fighting among the Italians and other ethnic immigrants. The violence of "gangsters" was part of my youth.

We had considerable violence in the past partly because many of the people came here from societies where disputes were often settled with violence. Vendettas, revenge, and events of that nature would bring out violent solutions. Violence is a threat, in our time, there is no doubt about it. This is aggravated by the legally protected freedom to own hand guns. On the other hand, the technology, the organization, and the management of the law enforcement agencies have significantly improved. Protection of lives and property has become a major industry in airports, offices, and homes.

Incidently, one area where there is a time bomb is in our prison system. When you look at crime, you have three aspects: the law enforcement system, the court system, and the penal system, or prisons. Heavy violence occurs in these places where there is suppression, restraint, and detention.

In places like Detroit, Miami, Washington or New York, there are some social strains in this time of transition that are putting great pressures on people which often stimulates violent situations. Sometimes violence is associated with poverty, frustration, lack of hope, or poor community institutions. I think that these unhealthy, violent places exist in almost every city that I have been in in the world. I do not think that there is, in the American social pattern, more violence than one would expect in a country where there are, for the great majority of people, systems for security, law and order.

In visiting, I think that you can feel safe in the United States. I would emphasize that one should take precautions in Washington the same as you would take if you went to Paris, London, Tokyo, Moscow, or New Delhi.

QUESTION 9

You blame our people for producing and supplying narcotics, marijuana, and these things to your country. But, if you didn't have so many psychologically disturbed people, so many drug addicts in the United States that create a market, we would not have a huge international drug problem. What is wrong with your society?

RESPONSE

There is no doubt that the social pressures and the cultural changes in the United States have brought addiction to such narcotics as hashish, cocaine, marijuana and heroin. They are part of a recent cultural change where alcohol is no longer the only form of substance abuse.

The problems of helping both individuals and societies that are corrupted by drug traffic is a very serious problem. It is an international problem to which the law enforcement agencies, courts, and penal institutions are trying desperately to find answers.

It is a very serious situation in all countries, when the least accountable and law-abiding elements drift into the narcotics traffic. There is some argument in the United States (stemming from American history where we had placed a law against the use and distribution of alcohol in the prohibition times of the 1920's and 1930's), that we should legalize marijuana and these various drugs and put them under legal distribution and control, as we did alcohol. There has been massive opposition to this by people who draw a distinction between the deleterious, addictive characteristics of drugs and those of alcohol. They say they are different. Other people do not draw a distinction between alcohol and drugs.

I see in my own city, community, and family the problems that can be created when young people seeking the pleasure of escape from the pressures of a highly competitive life turn to things such as marijuana, which they consider legitimate and much less harmful than alcohol. There is no doubt that we have created a market that is highly profitable for the syndicates, drug merchants, and drug producers of the world. It has become a major import/export business. We have sought with our laws, governmental agencies, and police mechanisms, both nationally and internationally, to check the flow of drugs, make distribution more difficult, and penalize those that are exploiting others through the drug trade.

Personally, I am sorry to see the influence of countries like Colombia that now have a major financial reliance on the income that is coming from the drug traffic. I think it is a corrupting element for other countries as well as for the United States. History shows some parallels in the "opium wars" of the past.

Again, this points to the fact that we are highly interdependent. The forces of law and order must cooperate today on an international basis, because the things happening in individual countries influence so many other people in other countries. I just hope that we can educate our people and our politicians, the people that have power in all societies, to cooperate in curtailing this very tragic and destructive trade.

Why do white people in America hate black people, Mexicans and other minorities?
RESPONSE

Sometimes we get these very blunt, generalized, implied criticisms. The fact is that white people do not "hate" blacks and Mexicans; by some standards some whites seem to hate blacks and Mexicans. Some whites also seem to hate Poles, and other kinds of people. Some blacks hate whites, and some Mexicans hate blacks. Here is where we get into a lot of stereotyping.

It is true that there are conflicts between interest groups in the society. They often do things that can be interpreted as hatred. For instance, I have a theory of what happened in the schools of Washington D.C. after the 1954 desegregation when white, middle-class children left Washington schools and started going to either private schools or schools in the suburbs. My conclusion is that it was not done because of hatred; it was done because of cultural fear. The white families were afraid that their children would start talking like the black children who they saw as poor, low-culture members of a society who spoke poor English, who had poor habits, etc. They were afraid that their children's futures would be jeopardized if they started talking like that, or if they started acting like the stereotypic poor black. Unfortunately, many of the whites never had contact with middle-class blacks, who were very much like they were and had the same type of fears. Many of the black middle-class also took their children out of the District schools. Consequently, there was a deterioration of the school system and a separation, in fact, of the races, with 91% of the District of Columbia school system now composed of black students.

It was not done out of hatred, although you could conclude that the whites hated the blacks and had won out. It was not hatred; it was really a fear and a concern that had nothing to do with hatred. The individual actions of these people in their relations with blacks were often very cordial and very cooperative. When you get these umbrella criticisms, "Why do you mistreat your wife?" or things like this, I think you have to separate them into specific cases.

Granted, there is some bigotry. Often you have fear and bias where you have ignorance. Fear engenders insecurity, intolerance, hatred, animosity, and aggression.

One of the great attempts that has been made in our country in the last 25 years has been the bringing together of people where they function together for their individual and mutual benefit. Equal opportunity statutes and regulations bring people together to cut down the fear, to reduce the differences, to bridge the cultural values gap between different kinds of people from, in a sense, different societies, even though they live in the same country.

It is a fallacy, however, to believe that if people understand each other better they will like each other better. That is not necessarily so; you may get to know people better and you may dislike them more. The thing to always keep in mind is that even though you dislike somebody and you may even fight with them, you can also negotiate with them and actually work with them when necessary. The American congress is a good example. Here is a situation where people coming together may know each other but may not like or trust each other; they may actually fight. But, you also have a situation where they respect and understand each other, where they can and must communicate and work together in the same national government. Discrimination exists in all societies. Social justice must be worked and fought for. The American civil rights movement is a dramatic example of such a fight in a free society.

QUESTION 11
Why are your Indians so bad off? Are they still being forced to live on reservations, and aren't they deprived of opportunities?
RESPONSE
Indians, or Native-Americans as they are often called, have a U.S. population of about 800,000 people. This is about the same sized population found at the time of the landing of the pilgrims back in the 1600's.

With the coming of the Europeans and other immigrants who forced the Indians out of their native habitats and hunting and living areas, the Indian population declined precipitously. Disease, warfare, and geographic displacement brought many losses to the Native-Americans. That population has reconstituted itself from maybe three or four hundred thousand back up to almost a million. According to tribal laws, you are an acknowledged American Indian or Native-American depending on what percentage of your ancestry is Native-American. Sometimes, if you are only one-eighth American Indian you qualify as a member of a tribe.

In some of the western states Indians live on tribal reservations that were established by treaty in the context of international law. In comparison with the immigrants, these people have lived on a primitive economic and social base, often in isolation. Unlike some of the other minorities, like the blacks and Hispanics who have been more effected by the modernization and change of these last hundred years, the Indian populations have been isolated in rural areas. So many times their opportunities have not been parallel to those of other minority groups.

The Indian reservations now exist primarily to keep the white or the non-Indian off of Indian land, not to keep the Indians on the reservation. They have the mobility and flexibility to leave anytime they want. In 1924, I believe it was, the Indians were given American citizenship, so they now have full voting and participation rights. However, they also have the protection and choice of living on reservations where they are subject to special provisions.

Admittedly, the white people who had power often tricked and exploited the Indians a hundred or a hundred and fifty years ago. But, don't blame me for what my grandfather's generation did to the Indians. I would not have done it, and many times people talk to me as if I am guilty. I am not. I do everything I can and will do anything I can do to bring equal opportunity, justice and fair play to all people in the United States. In my grandfather's generation, there were some pretty violent, designing, and sometimes exploitive and ambitious people.

Remember, too, that these new early settlers had come from Europe for a chance, opportunity, and safety. Suddenly they found that they had to fight for the land with the people that had been on the land before them. A lot of things were done because of hatred, bloodshed, insecurity, and warfare. There were no rules of the game; there was no peace, law, nor order. So a lot of the interaction between the Indians and the immigrants was a warfare situation where there was great injustice, hatred, and violence on all sides.

Fortunately that period is past, but the residue of that period has lingered. Many times these rural people have not had the education and system of motivation that would enable them to take advantage of the many opportunities that have become available. They may not have known about them. I would say that maybe 60% of the Indians are still on reservations.

In recent times oil and uranium have been found on some of these reservations. Some tribes are fantastically wealthy and have had meteoric rises similar to oil-rich countries in terms of their resources, educational patterns, and living standards. Still, there are an inordinant number of health, educational, and social problems because they are still in a developing, less productive stage in their society.

I think one thing that should be pointed out here is that many of the treaties that were dictated by the whites were treaties that, in effect, moved the Indian populations thousands of miles into desolate, unproductive, and strange areas that were alien to their whole culture and being. It is paradoxical that they are now finding oil and uranium in some of these areas, because these were the desolate, desert areas that no one else wanted.

There have been many programs, government and non-government, to try to help the Indian populations bridge cultural as well as economic and political gaps. Still, the predominant picture is that of an ethnic minority group that is basically underprivileged. It is definitely a very serious problem that has many economic, social and legal manifestations.

QUESTION 12

Do you think another Catholic (like Kennedy) could be elected President? Aren't most of your people anti-Catholic?
RESPONSE

I think another Catholic might be elected President, as was John Fitzgerald Kennedy. His personal skill and the appropriateness of his actions and style to his time made it possible for him to become president even though the majority of Americans were not Catholic.

I would say almost the same thing could happen to a black person, and even a little more remotely, to a woman. A person who has real charisma and a history of service and experience within the political power structure could transcend the prejudice in this system as Kennedy did. The Democratic party has been the traditional haven for organized Catholic power, and they, of course, have passed out of power. I do not see any person except Ted Kennedy, on the immediate horizon, who is Catholic and also active on the national political scene.

There has been a revitalizing of the political energy of the protestants. We have seen it in the Moral Majority and some of the fundamentalist movements in the various protestant groups. They might set up some competition if a Catholic began to surface as a candidate. Still, the Catholic Church is the largest single religious denomination in the United States. It has very persuasive powers. However, members do not all vote together; sometimes Catholics or Jewish people vote against Catholic or Jewish candidates. This is one example of a pluralistic society. While possible, I do not foresee in the immediate future a Catholic, black person, or woman becoming President of the United States, given the present voting patterns and personalities now on the political stage.

35

QUESTION 13

Are you Americans really informed? Many of your cities have only one newspaper and the owner also owns the T.V. or radio stations. Most of your news in America comes from very superficial television. It is so superficial you may get no real news at all. You can go months without seeing anything about important countries like Germany, Japan, Nigeria, Brazil, Turkey or India.

RESPONSE

If somebody asks me, "Aren't Americans poorly informed?" my first instinct is to agree, when compared with the news coverage in many other countries I have been in. Over 64% of Americans get their information from television broadcasts. The transcript of a 30-minute TV program would fit on the first page of the New York Times.

Our television and often our newspapers are really commercially designed to get readership and audience attention. Therefore, they often emphasize the dramatic more than informative or educational content. Criticism that there has been a news monopoly in the United States, with some cities having only one major newspaper, is often heard. Sometimes, ownership of the television, radio, and newspaper is all in the same hands. I think there certainly is some truth to this. But I also am very familiar with the quantity of information that is available to those people that want it and need it.

I guess I get something like nineteen different publications, ranging all the way from American publications on international affairs to European publications put out by the European community, to the Organization of American States publications on Latin America. I get the World Marxist Review, giving me continual insights into things that are happening from the point of view of communist societies. I receive a tremendous flow of information, much more than I can handle.

Even so, newspapers and television highlight many things for me. Specialized news sources today have been the great change in the media. Most people are getting national news from T.V. Local newspapers are commercial vehicles for advertising and for carrying community news. There has been more and more of a migration of news to the small communities in community papers. For instance, here in the District of Columbia, the Washington Post has supplements for neighboring communities, such as Montgomery County. They put in specialized news and advertising sections. I get Time magazine, and they distribute that on a regional basis where advertising in a certain section of Time is delivered to a part of the country and is dedicated to companies and organizations in that part of the country. It is specialized, localized advertising.

There are often anti-trust suits when the media seems to be monopolized by certain interests. There are also steps being taken by the government in the licensing of radio and T.V. (each requires a license from the Federal Communications Commission). There is still some truth to the fact that people perhaps are not as well informed as they should be where the media ownership is concentrated. However, the editorial policy, coverage, and style are different, even when you have two media with the same ownership.

By and large, there has been a fantastic growth of alternative sources of information: specialized publications and specialized programs. Moreover, the spread of cable television is going to further erode the monopoly as it brings as many as twenty channels into a community—in contrast to the two, three or four that have existed up to now. Again, with a dynamic problem, there is some truth to this criticism. But there are also some countervailing forces.

In brief, Americans who wish to be informed have access to excellent sources of information, ranging from the New York Times to specialized newsletters and journals that are available by computer. The general public, however, is underinformed, and I lament that.

QUESTION 14

Why don't the people from the United States living in our country mix with our people? You live in "capitalistic ghettos" and do not bother to learn our customs and our language.
RESPONSE

This question often comes up in connection with the seeming insularity of Americans when they go to other countries. I have heard the criticism many times that the Americans do not mix, that they act superior, do not learn the language, and are not really interested in other countries.

First of all, Americans sent overseas often find that the working language in the country is English. In Pakistan, for example, educated people speak English much better than an American could ever speak Urdu in the amount of time he/she would have to study it. Many organizations and companies will not spend that investment to teach their employees Urdu when they do not absolutely need it to do the business that they are there to do.

There is another element. When people are under pressure, working in a strange environment, and often working very hard because of insufficient help, thereby reducing efficiency, they are very tired at the end of a workday. There is a tendency, even with the best intentions, to try to relax and gather strength. Often you can only do this with somebody that speaks your language, understands you, eats your food, and with whom you can relax.

In Washington, D.C., you should see the "national-islands" after six o'clock at night. There is a Russian-speaking island, as well as Spanish-speaking, Arabic-speaking, Dutch-speaking, German-speaking, and Italian-speaking islands. People from the embassies, multinational companies, World Bank, and other organizations retreat to their language or cultural islands to eat, socialize, and find necessary relaxation in comfort.

So, it is a natural phenomenon for people of any country, particularly under the pressure of working overseas today, to group into cliques.

Also, for many countries we have had to offer the Americans a higher standard of living to entice them to even leave the United States. We have to pay them more than they would get in the United States and include servants and facilities that they do not need when they are living in the United States.

Foreign employees working for the American government here often ask, "Why is it that Americans are so much different when we meet them at home in the United States than when they are in our country where they often act like VIP's or special people?" It is not that they want to act like "special people," but when they are overseas (for instance, working with the government) they are usually assigned to work with certain kinds of people—usually the elite, usually in the government or academic community. Those are the people with whom they spend their time.

So many people say "Aha! See, they are not interested in the people. They are just spending time with the big shots, or the politicians, or the powerful people." Well, it happens that they are sent overseas to work in programs that deal with those people and not necessarily with the masses of people. This tends to isolate them from people who, by and large, are not in a position of power, or don't have the resources or money.

Of course, one great contrast are groups such as the Peace Corps. We also have a Retired Executives' Service Corps, the Christian Service Corps, many volunteer organizations, CARE and other organizations which have carried Americans overseas to live with the people, no matter what their condition. They are spread out with non-prestige, non-elite groups. So we have examples of both; but this question often does come up.

We have to admit that sometimes insecure people abuse the power they get, and do act in an arrogant, haughty, or condescending way. I might also add another psychological factor that I have noticed. When people have an inferiority complex, they often compensate for it by assuming superiority behavior. And when people confront challenges they do not understand, such as often happens while living in another country, they will go there and be condescending, patronizing and intolerant to cover up their own insecurity and their own weakness.

So yes, the practical effects of this are that some people act arrogantly. They are often the people who are the least equipped, prepared, and sensitive. Still, things may be less critical than they used to be.

QUESTION 15

Why do your people know so little about us and our country? You know nothing about our people, our cities, our politics, our government. Doesn't this really prove that Americans are not interested in anybody else, especially our country?

RESPONSE

This is a very frequent observation made by people from all parts of the world, even when they come here or read American publications, or see on television a small item about their country. And they also talk to Americans coming to their country and find out how little they often know about the people that they are visiting.

Communication and media are basic aspects of American life. This huge country is somewhat self-contained. We have busy and demanding individual lives. There is so much that we are exposed to with huge newspapers, radio, television, educational systems, and books. Yet, there is only so much attention one can maintain.

I have found that Americans are generally aware of other countries only as they are high-lighted in the media during a crisis. If it does not directly influence American life or American interest, they just do not take the time to learn about it. They also often fail to keep up with what is happening in different parts of their own country.

The United States impacts on many other countries economically, socially, politically, and culturally, because of its power, outreach, and influence. The United States has an effect on almost every country of the world. The lives of Americans are not reciprocally influenced by actions of all other countries.

Everyone is looking at us out of their own national or self interest. For example, someone in Colombia says, "You do not know anything about Colombia. Look at your TIME Magazine: Maybe once a year you have three paragraphs about Colombia in the magazine." The fact is that TIME Magazine may get a ten-page report every week from their correspondent in Colombia but, because of competition for space, they may only print two or three paragraphs. Two or three paragraphs may be better than nothing. In the United States, unless it is a crisis or something of broad interest, Colombia may have relatively little impact, interest, or effect on the average American reader and thus be neglected by the competitive media.

The reverse is true for many Colombians who may know relatively more about the United States than many American citizens. They may know more about the United States than Americans will know about their own country because certain things in the United States are likely to be more essential to them personally, and to their country.

Another factor to consider is that there is less attention to world history, geography, and memorizing places and dates, for example, in the American school system. The American student is apt to be taking driver training instead of learning history and geography because those seem to be more relevant to the parents and to those who set up the curriculum. Another aspect of this is the pattern of American history which has brought people into a land isolated by two oceans, where the whole attention was focused on the continent. Isolationism, in other words, was somehow programmed into the American style. I must add that in my travels to many countries, I have found the 'average' citizens knew and cared little about international affairs.

QUESTION 16

I'm quite interested in sending my boy to America to study, but many people say that your schools neglect the fundamentals; they neglect the discipline and the culture, things that are so important. Your modern facilities are beautiful, but your people don't use them, the students never take advantage of these things. I think that the British school system is much better, don't you really think so?
RESPONSE

There is a major concern over these issues in the American community. For instance, much work is being done to upgrade the quality of our public schools. Yet, we have had our problems. Consider some of the undeniable losses of quality education that have come from racial integration of schools. While integration is desireable, we have not yet overcome the problems of such a drastic social transformation.

When the black school system and the white school system, which were not equal, were put together, many times the qualities of each suffered. What happened often was that the middle class whites moved to the suburbs, deserting the inner city schools. Many of the quality teachers left to follow better paying jobs and better working conditions. The results have been most unfortunate. The District of Columbia school system, which is now 91% black, is having some very difficult times, not just in questions of salaries, but in questions of quality, discipline, and all of the things that you asked in the question.

This is also a problem in the suburban high schools. Much of the focus and attention of the education process has been shifted from the school to outside the school, to television and also a very educated, enriched environment that takes much of the student's attention. A permissive society has often emphasized entertainment and "being happy" rather than being prepared, disciplined, and trained in how to operate in a highly competitive economic and political society.

So, there is a lot of truth to your question. There are many problems in the educational community. There may be some validity to the idea that the elite school systems in Europe probably do give a much more general educational foundation than the public school systems here. Nevertheless, our well-organized public schools are very effective. They are made good by good teachers, good financing by the community, support from Parent Teacher Associations, research and enrichment programs. But in many of the inner city schools, where many of these things do not exist, the public schools are not very effective.

One thing that has balanced this situation is the fantastic increase of post high school education. In my youth, if you did not get into college by age 20, you probably were not going to college. Today, it is completely different. It developed with the "GI Bill of Rights" which made it possible for many people who did not really have the money to go to college to get funding from the government in partial compensation for their military service. That is the way I got to law school. I personally could not have afforded my graduate work otherwise. That meant opening the colleges and universities to adults as well as youth. There are eleven million people in our colleges and universities. The door is open to people of all ages.

Often at the secondary level the quality is not very good, but there are compensations. People who are serious and want the education, people of varied economic groups can get into college—perhaps later in their career after they have had work experience. The quality of American postgraduate education is generally considered the best in the world. The presence of over 300,000 international students in American colleges and universities is evidence of the positive reputation of American higher education.

There is considerable truth to the statement that problems exist in America's school system. Fortunately, it is one of the areas where we are diligently working. There are exciting things being done with computer training, efforts to better train and bring technology to bear in the learning process and in the preparation of teachers.

Education is perhaps the second largest industry in the United States. And in that industry there are fantastic resources that are available to the masses.

QUESTION 17

Why is it that Americans do not have strong philosophies and spiritual convictions? I expect that it is because you are such pragmatic, materialistic people. You do not have the spirit and the soul for philosophy or for conceptualizing profound ideas and principles.

RESPONSE

I have had this said to me in many ways by Europeans, Asians and by people in many parts of the world who see Americans as just "doers." I think of de Toqueville's observation about the kinds of people that settled this country. And when you look at it, yes we had our Jeffersons, and we had our Hamiltons. We had an elite that came over from Europe, principally from England but also from France and other countries. We had landowners, educated people, second and third sons of powerful families, even royal families. But, by and large, the people that settled this country were not the intellectuals, nor the bourgoisie, nor the aristocracy. The great numbers of people came to the U.S. seeking opportunity, without any notoriety. They were often from the peasant class or religious minority groups. Others were indentured servants who had been in trouble at home and were trying for a new start. Many more had been persecuted or pushed out of their countries. Some came as slaves.

I remember hearing various stories taken from the Italian and Yugoslav campaigns during World War II where the United States would drop Italian-Americans or Yugoslav-Americans behind the lines. They were often American officers. When they would meet the partisans, many of whom had been fighting fascists or the Nazis, it was quite a shock. The partisans were often leaders and people with a good education in their countries. They would meet these Italian-Americans or Yugoslav-Americans who were college-educated officers, but who could only speak the peasant dialects of Italy and Yugoslavia because their parents and grandparents had been peasants or from lower classes. Their ancestors had emigrated for a new chance in America.

Many of this kind of basic stock were refugees from Northern Europe in the initial waves and then later from Southern Europe and other continents. These people often were not professed intellectuals, nor were they thinkers or synthesizers. They were doers. They worked very hard to get basic material security. Generation after generation they worked to build a better life. This usually included a better standard of living, and more education, wealth, opportunity, and sophistication.

Today, the United States does not take a back seat in the academic or intellectual community to any country in the world. I make no apology for the outstanding work that is being done in our research institutes and intellectual communities. There is real quality in the probing research and study in the social sciences that makes profound philosophic, spiritual, and psychological contributions.

On the other hand, it is true that pragmatic Americans, particularly businessmen, interact with foreigners on a practical basis. They are often specialists dealing with educated Europeans who are often generalists. In their education the European counterparts have spent much time than the average American studying history, philosophy, and culture. The more broadly educated European may feel disdain for the American who has spent more time developing specialized knowledge. There is often the impression that the American is not very philosophic, nor idea-oriented. Certainly for large numbers of Americans that may be true. Sophistication, however, is usually relative.

I might make one more comment here on the "spiritual and religious." During the 1960's there was a great social revolution against the "establishment" and materialism by American youth. This was when we had the "flower children," the "hippies," and many young people who felt that there should be more philosophy and spirituality. They carried it to an extreme. Now there is a return from that sort of "going back to the native" and the non-material. Society could not operate at the productive level that people demanded when too much time and effort went to the contemplative or spiritual.

On the other hand, many people are saying, "We've gotten too materialistic; we've gone away from our God; we've gone away from our religion; let's get back to the basic morality and basic value system that our religions gave us." I think this is a very healthy trend as long as we preserve the rich diversity and pluralism of the society. As you saw in the American election of 1980, people organized to develop a political force as well as a spiritual force to increase the spiritual and moral content of the activities in society and the quality of life in the United States.

QUESTION 18

Why do you send such bad movies and television programs to our country which corrupt our youth and also hurt the American reputation?

RESPONSE

This whole problem, this question about the exportation of bad American movies has been going on for fifty years. Now, we also have bad American TV being exported.

The fact is, in a competitive society, the good and the bad are available for export. Many of us working in information and cultural programs have lamented this. Still, X-rated movies and pornography are pouring out of Europe and the United States into some of these areas where motion pictures and television are often an escape from the harsh realities of life in a low-income society.

This is a very serious problem that I think most Americans justly lament. Yet, as we discuss this we need to remember some of the constructive things that are sent out to help the educational systems upgrade their access to resources, computerized data, and quality information. As a matter of record, part of the justification for our information and cultural programs in the U.S. Information Agency, Fulbright programs, teacher exchanges, and university programs, is trying to counteract and to get quality exchange counterbalancing the material that is exported in the amusement market, often by irresponsible distributors. Cultural programs are designed to do much of the same thing on a cooperative basis.

QUESTION 19

Aren't you Americans really weak because you are getting almost everything you need without really working for it? You think this jogging, this ridiculous jogging, people running around for no purpose, is going to really help you? Why not put your energies into more meaningful purposes?
RESPONSE

Here is an example of an American "easy life" image. Some estimates I have seen say that maybe 25% of the American people are overweight. It is interesting to me that we have had sort of a reversal of history in this country. All through history, in Asia and Europe, one of the signs of being powerful and wealthy was being fat, big, and obese. It is interesting here that in the wealthier upper classes, the people spend a great deal of money, time, and energy keeping trim, exercising, keeping in the best of health, eating wholesome foods and taking vitamins.

Now this is something that has attained mass popularity. Jogging, which I have seen develop just in the last 4 or 5 years, is a mass activity. People began to see that they were getting soft because they were going everyplace in automobiles and not walking. There were more people working at desks and computer consoles. And TV has taken its toll.

So, we have almost developed a cult of conditioning that may look ridiculous. But we are seeing that performance tests in schools are showing that this new conditioning and exercise are beginning to improve the physical tone of Americans as they use their muscles and participate more. But, this is still a continuing problem. Technology, automobiles, TV, and elevators all present appealing alternatives to physical activity.

It is interesting to me that the obese people I see now are often in the poverty areas, in the inner city. They eat junk food, their diets are inadequate, they do not exercise adequately, and they eat compulsively, often out of frustration. Particularly, I see this with women in poverty areas where the demands and pressures of their situation frustrate them, as does lack of group activities. For example, taking care of many children often drives them into compulsive eating.

Yes, many Americans have been getting soft, but they have recognized it and have taken some very interesting steps. Note the tremendous growth in such athletic activities as gymnastics, aerobics, slimnastics, tennis, and various group sports and exercises. There has been an amazing sports revival here. The growth of sports can be noted even in industry. This is a very dynamic thing, but in this individualistic society it is a question of personal choice.

People not only have the freedom to be soft, but they also have the freedom to take care of themselves. Millions of people are getting the message that they should take better care of their own lives. More evidence that they are heeding this message is, for instance, the decrease in death from heart attacks. Many people are not only stopping smoking, but they are doing things that will improve the vitality of their systems and lower their susceptibility to heart attacks.

Section II:
American Government

The political institutions and practices of almost any country will seem strange to its foreign visitors on at least some counts. Nowhere is the curiousness of outside observers more aroused, however, than when they first confront what are the unusually unique aspects of American political history and institutions. And, when they try to interpret the forms and practices of our government from the vantage of experience with their own system of government, they are often confused or even taken-back by our political traditions.

Ours is a different political system on numerous counts. To some we overindulge ourselves in the pursuit of human justice and human rights at the cost of efficiency in governmental administration. To others, we have not gone far enough in assuring civil liberties. To some we are too willing to allow openly expressed dissent. To others the reverse propensity is perceived. To some the "Freedom of Information Act" is an overindulgence of the rights of citizens to monitor their government, while our historic shortcomings in coping with minority and ethnic rights are seen as inhumane. To many, ours is a system of much diversity or even contradictory political practices.

We might do well, then, to communicate that ours is a complex society composed of diverse social groupings with ancestries in a great variety of nations, cultures, and experience. The coming together of these diverse traditions has produced a most interesting mix, politically as well as culturally. Moreover, we are a relatively "young" nation. Ours is not a system with institutional residues from the period of kings, princes, and absolute monarchs. Nor was our political system the creation of landed aristocrats attempting to maintain a position of power and influence in the face of peasant rebels. Liberty and equality were ideals given fertile soil in the relatively recent birth of our nation. But, neither have we been negligent in establishing political entities with the authority to govern. Private liberty has not gone untempered by awareness of collective or public interests.

Consequently, our political system is a "mixed" system. Government governs, and often quite vigorously. When it disallows certain groups what they perceive to be their due rights, then our political heritage seems to not only allow, but invite dissent. Public institutions attempt to curtail abuses born of the pursuit of private interest, and private interests collaborate to avert excesses in government's attempts to set norms and guidelines in areas thought better left to private discretion. Perhaps we can best help those asking questions about our political system by suggesting that American democracy rests upon a conscious attempt to promote this dynamic interplay of competing interest. Any citizen or group of citizens can make demands on our political leaders and/or institutions. These competing demands are openly invited; great effort is made to allow diversity in the political process. Yet, out of these diverse demands, compromises are fashioned and a set of relatively satisfactory mores and traditions have emerged giving the American system significant stability.

We should also recognize that at times in our history the "political experiment" has brought less than desirable outcomes. Ours is not a political history without its dark side. Shameful periods and practices all too frequently dot the landscape of our political history. Yet, hopefully, we have remained open to the competing demands and philosophies of a diverse population. Competition among ideas and political philosophies has been allowed, while political parties and other political institutions have helped us determine, via compromise and common consent, what works here.

We need not downplay the vitality of our political system. Ours is a heritage of which we are rightfully proud. At the same time, we would do well to recognize that others can rightfully criticize us on numerous counts. Why not admit to our shortcomings, illustrate our attempts to alter our political institutions to remedy those weaknesses, and thereby embody in our answers the same kind of openness to diverse opinion that is at the heart of the American political heritage. We can acknowledge the insights implicit in the expressions of those with whom we interact within or from other lands, without belittling the richness of our own political experience and institutions. We can be understanding of their perceptions of our political system while also giving substantively rich insights that might clarify certain misperceptions that they might hold.

QUESTION 20

In watching your 1980 elections, I did not really see the difference between your Democratic Party and Republican Party. What is the difference? Where did Anderson fit in?
RESPONSE

I often find myself trying to explain our political system to people from countries all over the world where politics are essentially ideological, or consist of a program or of a personality in power. Usually we see others running from the extreme left (communist) to the extreme right (fascist). The parties in the United States, as they have historically developed, are sort of umbrella parties.

They go from left to right in both parties. We have a situation where conservatives in the Democratic Party and conservatives in the Republican party are just about the same conservatives, except that they are in a different part of the country, or are from a different historical development in a given state, or are from a city where their parties had their particular historic roots.

Traditionally in the United States we find that about 41 percent of the American voters are Democrats. We find that about 22 or 23 percent are Republicans, while the rest may vote Democratic or Republican, or register Democratic or Republican. In fact, they are actually Independents who vote either on the issue or the personality involved, not out of any party loyalty.

Fervent membership and discipline are lacking in the Republican and Democratic parties in the United States. To become a Democrat or a Republican and to be eligible to vote all you have to do is register with the local government. Some Republicans and Democrats contribute to their chosen party and have a sort of contribution card, but there is no membership card as such. There are some active Republican and Democratic membership organizations, but in general terms the membership is very loose, informal, and often only nominal.

Also, it is quite obvious that millions of Democrats voted for President Eisenhower, President Nixon and President Reagan, because there were not enough declared Republicans to elect them.

In recent years the differences between the parties in very general terms have been that the Democrats have been more in favor of public sector development and governmental solutions to national and international problems. This is partly because the main coalition that gave strength to the Democrats from the Franklin Roosevelt period to the present was made up of labor groups, minority groups, and intellectuals. In the American political spectrum, these people tended to be to the "left," or to the side of collective and governmental activity. More people in the Republican party have tended to emphasize private enterprise, individual effort, and less government control and regulation.

These are only very broad generalizations; often there are few ideological differences. Often there is more difference within the parties. In fact, one thing that often surprises people from other countries, particularly from parliamentary systems, is that during some fights in the Congress you find Republicans and Democrats voting together against another coalition of Republicans and Democrats. The congressmen are voting, supposedly, to represent their voters' or constituents' needs at home. If they are from a farm constituency or an industrial constituency, they may vote in the interest of their supporters instead of down a Republican or Democratic party line.

Now in the 1980 election, Anderson was a phenomenon. He did not represent a party. He represented a potential Republican candidate who found that he was not going to be able to get the nomination of the Republican party in competition with Mr. Reagan. So he broke off and began an independent personal campaign for the presidency, and he succeeded in getting seven per cent of the popular vote, although he got no electoral votes, which is what really elects the president in our indirect election system. There have been other third parties. Most people do not realize that in this pluralistic political system we actually have a Communist party, a Socialist party, a Socialist-Workers party, a Vegetarian party, a Prohibition party, and a Libertarian party. We have many different parties representing many different special interests. But, because of the traditional political configurations, with very few exceptions these parties have no national office holders and few local or state office holders. In general terms they have not been successful in getting the popular vote or financial or power base to challenge the two major political parties.

QUESTION 21

How can a peanut farmer and a movie actor even try to get the presidency? What were their qualifications? We should have experienced people in positions with as much power in the world as the American president has. How do these people get elected?

RESPONSE

I think that the American electoral system is a puzzlement to many people in other countries where the political parties are usually ideological and/or personality parties with leaders who have been in party power for years and years. By contrast you have the situation in the United States where a man like President Carter can be elected. However, he certainly was and is a lot more than a peanut farmer. He was a career naval officer and a nuclear engineer, and as the governor of Georgia was the administrator of one of the most complicated and fastest growing state organizations in the United States.

Still, he performed a political miracle as a relatively unknown governor, unknown on the national scene. In twenty-two months he became well known by traveling, working, and broadcasting, and by his communicating ideas in a well organized campaign to get the nomination of his party. Then he beat President Ford who was an incumbent president.

Ronald Reagan is quite well known to the world community because of his motion picture experience. But very few people are really conscious of the long, political career of this man. He started out as a Democrat in the opposition party to the party that he now represents, the Republican party. He was a union leader as head of the Screen Actors Guild at a very difficult time in the history of union organizations in the 30's and 40's. Over the years he was in politics, supporting various candidates and then actively campaigning within the Republican party as he was moving into national recognition.

For the last three national conventions of the Republican party, he was a serious contender as a Presidential candidate for the conservative wing of the Republican party. This was based on his extensive experience as a broadcaster in radio, as a commentator, as a writer, and as a governor (as was Carter). He was governor of the largest state in the United States, which in economic terms would rank as the tenth most powerful nation in the world if California were an independent nation.

He served two terms as governor, being re-elected with many of the same criticisms that came up during the campaign for his election for president. Many claimed that he was extremely conservative, that he was prone to "shoot from the hip," that he was an ideologist and not a practical politician and that he did not have political experience.

51

After serving as governor of California, Reagan spent almost three years combing the United States, going to every segment, every state, supporting and rebuilding the Republican party after Watergate and the Nixon period which had so seriously damaged the reputation of the Republican Party.

In 1980, Reagan enjoyed a resounding victory. He got about ten million more votes than Mr. Carter did, as well as many more electoral votes in our indirect election system.

How does a man like this get elected? First of all, he has to work and then work some more to get the support necessary for the nomination as the candidate of his party. Now 36 of our 50 states have primary elections where they elect the delegates to the national party convention that chooses the Presidential candidate of the major parties. He has to get party support and financing. He has to be able to meet every kind of interest group and every kind of audience, and gain support and recognition from the media. So, being elected is a very complicated economic, social, political, emotional and collective enterprise.

For example, President Carter and President Reagan won by hard work, duty, and service to their parties, and by putting together rather remarkable teams that worked on local, county, state, regional and national levels. Not only did the teams work with people but with issues and communication skills since TV, mass media and emotions affect public opinion and voting decisions so much. Much power has passed from party political leaders to communication and campaign specialists who can "produce the vote."

They did all this within the dynamics of the domestic American political system. They were often working down in the "grassroots," as they say, "down with the voter." These people worked at the basic roots of their parties, building support that produced an election campaign organization capable of getting the votes necessary to help them become President.

So, "How does a person become President?" Not just anybody can become president. It has to be somebody with experience, a party record, significant service and organization, and major amounts of hard, long, continuous team work. It is possible to be a relative newcomer, in terms of national politics, but you will never find a person getting to the presidential position who does not have substantial political and government experience, party organization, and an organization that can get the money necessary in a modern campaign to compete effectively and win.

QUESTION 22

Who makes policy in the United States now? Presidents Johnson, Nixon, Ford and Carter made agreements and your congress turned them down. And now it is doing the same thing to President Reagan. How can we negotiate with you? How can we depend on you?

RESPONSE

I wish I had a chalkboard to draw a diagram that I have used to describe who makes foreign policy in the United States. Of course, the answer is that it depends on what policy it is, what you are talking about, what time it is, and who is in power. In general terms, the responsibility for foreign policy lies with the President of the United States and his officers in the executive branch.

But we know in practice that many policies have, in effect, been made by Congress. Still, Congress and the President may lay down the laws, the executive orders, and the treaties, but policy is often made by the people carrying out the policy, namely, the ambassadors and the bureaucrats who are interpreting the policy. Policies may be made by a Congressional staff member who writes an amendment after the policy has been established, limiting how it can be carried out. Policy may also be made by special interest groups and lobbyists and by allies who try to affect the decisions of diplomats, the people in the State Department, or the people in Congress.

Policy has been made recently by events. Who ever dreamed that the Olympics would be influenced by an unpredicted move of the Russians into remote Afghanistan? Events, often magnified by the media, influence public opinion, which in turn influences the bureaucrats and Congress who may alter a policy in a very short time. The 1973 Arab-Israeli war affected the economic, social, political and financial policies of almost every country in the world. Events often completely change the plans and the designs of the people who have power. So, who makes American policy? The formal making of American policy is in the hands of the President and his officers in the executive branch. However, since support money generally has to be provided by Congress, ways are found in the legislative branch for modifying that exercise of power. The agreements, particularly the treaties, made by the executive branch are subject to the ratification, advice, and consent of the Senate. And then, special interest groups who have provided political support for the party or the officers in power may influence the decisions that are made and the implementation or carrying out of policy.

In certain issues, particularly those dealing with the Soviet Union, normalization of economic relations, human rights concerns, and things of this nature, some policies and agreements are even revised by Congress. For example, there are cases where President Carter had taken specific action, signed treaties such as SALT (the Strategic Arms Limitation Treaty), and embraced Mr. Brezhnev in Vienna, only to find that the Congress would not ratify the treaty.

In this new Administration, President Reagan has stated that he did not support the SALT Treaty and he would not urge that it be ratified. He would open the door to new negotiations. I think that there are indications that the Soviets have accepted this policy change.

So who makes policy? I still have to come back to the fact that it is made by different people at different times, all the way from the bureaucrats to the President. I think you have to investigate each issue by looking at special interests in and out of the government, American and non-American. They work hard to influence policy. You can analyze who actually influences policy on a specific issue at a specific time.

QUESTION 23

Isn't it true that American businesses, the monopolies, the multinational corporations, are really the ones that determine American foreign policy in your country? Aren't the military industrialists and the scientists the ones that really are controlling American foreign policy around the world?
RESPONSE

A common criticism of the United States is that the multinational corporations, the military industrial cliques and the Zionists (American Jews) have a monopoly on American power. I perceive that no group has an enduring monopoly on American power. However, certain people and certain groups can sometimes concentrate their power for a limited time and get extraordinary influence.

For instance, during certain periods of our history the Zionists exploited their contacts within the American Jewish community. With a concentrated effort they were able to influence certain policies and programs.

In the Middle East conflict today, however, they would have much less power to control events and public opinion than they had in the past. Now many Arab-American organizations, oil companies, and parts of the American public (horrified by the massive Israeli bombings of West Beirut) would rise to challenge or to question Israeli influence in the American government actions and policies in the Middle East. There is a balancing of pressure groups taking place.

Ours is a corrective society. If suddenly labor gets too much power it seems that business, the public and government stop fighting among themselves, come together, and counterbalance labor. This is Galbraith's concept of "countervailing forces." If one element of the society tends to get too much power, other elements will cooperate, even if they do not like each other, to bring back equilibrium and a balance of power. This balance of power exists. However, there is no doubt that under certain conditions a big corporation may be able to influence a certain policy until it becomes obvious that it is either corrupt or prejudicial to other interest groups in the United States.

When we analyze American foreign policy we have to look at basic conditions that influence policy, such as national security and economic or prosperity concerns of the nation. Some of our policies are influenced by a tradition of humanism, of helping people. Our policy today is also influenced at any given time by varying combinations of special interest groups. On one issue these groups may be fighting, on another issue they may be cooperating. Another thing has changed the United States foreign policy making process. Since Vietnam and Watergate the presidency has lost considerable power in foreign affairs. That power has gone to Congress, which itself is much more diversified, individualistic, and undisciplined.

Consequently, we have a diverse mix, but nobody has a monopoly. A dynamic interchange of power influences American foreign policy, as does the dynamic interplay of the bureaucracy of the American government itself.

QUESTION 24

How can you let public servants strike—your teachers, farmers, truck drivers, and police? Strikes can create chaos in America. How can you have control if everybody is doing their own thing?

RESPONSE

The right to strike is considered and has been judged in American courts as one of the fundamental rights in our American-type of democracy. However, there are laws where certain groups can be stopped by court order if national security and public safety are jeopardized.

We have had quite a few examples in recent history of teachers striking. Incidently, they usually go on strike at the beginning of the school year and delay the opening of the school year. When the teachers strike, the supervisors often cover school operations during the negotiations.

We have had a rather limited number of strikes by the police and fire forces in some of our big cities. In strikes during the last two years, there have been examples of destruction during the time that a fire department's work was temporarily covered by the national guard, or by volunteers and supervisors who were inadequate for that responsibility.

Such chaos is often counterbalanced in our society. Once a strike, founded on a just or good cause, gets to the point where both sides are losing, the public puts on pressure, and negotiations are finally successful. In the public interest, sometimes the governor or the mayor will step in with emergency measures until negotiations are finally successful, and agreement and settlement of the strike takes place.

It is my observation that as people get more options and alternatives, and as they perceive more ways of solving problems, it is more and more difficult to be a dictator, whether it is a dictator in a home, city, or country. One of the effective ways that can stand up to authoritarianism, exploitation and injustice, is by the collective action of a strike. Very elaborate contract arrangements have been made in labor laws, negotiation procedures, and arbitration agreements for both public servants and people in private industry. Also, there are ways for meeting meaningful grievances and having these things adjudicated and acted upon, hopefully short of a strike. But if a strike is necessary, it should be within the legal bounds of a strike, without violence and destruction.

When you consider the number of conflicting interests, the unbelievable pressures created today by inflation, problems of keeping a delicate balance between balancing budgets, and meeting needs of people for increased salaries, it is a miracle that there have not been more strikes. But, there is an exceptional appreciation on the part of American leadership that there must be a responsible balance struck lest the interests of both sides be basically defeated and damaged.

Other countries, of course, have had this problem also. I have been in countries where student strikes have paralyzed an entire school system, even in a country like Japan. I have seen this personally in places like Pakistan. I have seen student strikes and teacher strikes, and occasionally police and public servant strikes. I believe this is a worldwide phenomena which is even spreading, as we have recently seen in Poland, to basically authoritarian countries. Such regimes today must be cognizant of legitimate grievances on the part of the people. They have so many alternate ways of operating and living today even in relatively closed and controlled societies.

My answer here is basically to affirm that these strikes have happened and have not caused undue chaos. But let's not make any mistake about it: these strikes, and the threat of these strikes, are a continuing and serious problem. In some states, the careers of students have been very seriously hurt by teacher strikes. The safety of communities has been jeopardized by firemen and police strikes. We probably will see more of these as tensions and economic stresses increase in a period of inflation and competition.

This is a very serious problem. I am not minimizing it. What I am saying is that, by and large, you need to consider the mechanisms of the American democracy that have allowed these strikes, while in some cases limiting them by judicial procedures if they truly endanger the public. These strikes have not produced chaos. They have preserved the right to strike and the instrumentality of negotiation that is so important in the democratic process.

QUESTION 25

With your Freedom of Information Act, and irresponsible officials and journalists who often reveal government secrets, how can you have good security for diplomacy and intelligence? Isn't the CIA useless now?

RESPONSE

This is a question that embodies a number of things, particularly in the minds of allies with whom we have security treaties, where intelligence is a very important part of defense cooperation.

This is a very practical problem. In a sense it is a paradox. After Vietnam and Watergate the Central Intelligence Agency got an excessive amount of publicity. Much of it was very negative and raised heavy criticism from people in America and in other countries. After Watergate there was a feeling that the government had to be more accountable.

Consequently, the Freedom of Information Act was passed several years ago, making it compulsory for the government to make information in government files available to American citizens asking for it, unless there were overriding security considerations.

This has created unbelievable demands on the bureaucracy to service these requests for information from personnel files, diverse records, and hearings in the government bureaucracy. Unfortunately, there have been some situations where there has been confusion about classifications and availability of information. Some security information or intelligence has been compromised.

There is another problem. There are leaks in government information systems. As a matter of fact, there is some evidence that some leaks have been made by the government to try to get some kind of idea about the reaction that might take place if some of the information in the leaks were true or were not true. It is said that President Johnson used to "leak" information to the media to test public reaction.

These are some of the dilemmas of working in an open, democratic society. There are people who feel they have a right to information, are suspicious of closed negotiations, and mistrust government officials who interact with people from other countries without revealing the source of their information or without revealing the fact that negotiations and activities are going on at all.

The CIA, however, is definitely not cancelled out. Their job is certainly more difficult; some types of their activities and operations have been very seriously curtailed or limited, both by publicity and legal requirements. There is a new consciousness that the government is responsible for what it does. It must be very careful not to infringe upon the rights, not only of the United States citizens and organizations, but of other sovereign peoples and countries.

I personally feel that the intelligence community is essential, not only the Central Intelligence Agency but also the Defense Intelligence Agency and the armed services intelligence activities, as well as the intelligence operations of the Federal Bureau of Investigation and other police forces. The intelligence function is necessary for almost all countries to obtain the facts necessary to make judgments and decisions that are important in an interdependent world. The press, media and other open sources of information just do not serve as reliably accurate sources of information needed for leadership and management of power.

The CIA is healthy. In the Reagan administration it will probably get more discretion and authority to conduct programs in the national interest and to remedy some of the handicaps that have recently been placed upon it.

QUESTION 26

Is it true that millions of people cannot afford medical care in your country? Why can't you have a government program where everybody can get health care with dignity?
RESPONSE

I think that there has been a tremendous change in the last few years in our tradition of private medicine. Consider welfare programs, Medicare,Medicaid supply, and medical care for indigent people and for older people either at highly subsidized rates or at no expense to the patient. This has been a major development towards filling in some gaps where people have not been able to afford decent medical care.

The other development, of course, has been the tremendous increase in the cost of medical care. This is partly because of inflation and partly because of increasing sophistication in hospital equipment and personnel skills that have added expenses in terms of technology, medicine, testing, therapeutic devices, and technology in the operating room.

In the past, much of the nursing was done by virtual peons or quasi-slave labor. Now, you no longer have the situation where most of the labor is supplied by religious workers, or by a poor, untrained, unorganized laboring class of people. The nurses, technicians, and service personnel are often highly trained and competent and they earn respectable professional salaries often obtained through collective bargaining.

For the majority of Americans, part of the medical expense has been taken care of by extensive systems of health insurance which are often partially paid for either by the employer, the government, and/or the employee. The great majority of Americans come under these protective systems. They often do fall financially short in cases of catastrophic illness or accident. Sometimes, government insurance or workman's compensation pays for some of the calamity.

In my own middle class family, no health care program, no insurance system could take care of an eight-month terminal cancer from which my father died. The immense medical bills that he incurred took a large part of our family resources. I have seen that tragedy in my own family, and I have seen it in many other families.

Senator Kennedy, among others, has been a leader in proposing legislation that would bring a form of nationalized medicine to the United States. This has been opposed by the American Medical Association and by many other groups that feel that the private practice of medicine is much more efficient and much more productive. I, myself, have mixed feelings.

I look at the good things and the bad things of, let's say, the Danish system, the Swedish system, the Australian system, and the British system. I have heard people from those countries criticize and praise their system. I think that in the next ten or fifteen, possibly even in the next five years, we will have some modified national health care program. This is because medical care is so expensive, and the benefits of this system are falling unequally among different groups of people. By and large, though, the standards of health, in both preventative and remedial help, the standards of our technology, innovation, research, medical care, and drugs, are bringing greater longevity, easing suffering and making great progress in the relief of human suffering.

With them, however, have come the problems of management, bureaucracy, and finance. This, again, is a very dynamic area in the American society. It has been fought over, economically, socially and politically. It is a very challenging situation where there are many problems to be solved. At the same time, there are many things of which we can be proud.

59

When you have a democratic constitution, why do your people have to fight for civil rights? If you're really a democracy, people should have their civil rights.

RESPONSE

This question is often raised, either in connection with America not practicing what it preaches, or relative to its emphasis on human rights. We would deny assistance to countries whose human rights standards do not meet the criteria or standards determined by Congress, the State Department, or the Administration. There has been a lot of resentment because Americans hold others to a certain standard of human rights and civil rights when many claim that the Americans themselves do not practice what they preach even in their own country.

There are certain standards in relation to terror and torture, denying people their physical liberty, and giving them access to the judicial systems, which are generally recognized by the United Nations and in almost all countries.

There has been much debate in the American government about the emphasis and the implementation of various policies on human and civil rights. Some people feel that the human rights include economic rights, where people have a right to a job and equality of living standards and results, as well as equal opportunity. In an open, pluralistic society, it is difficult to insure equal results when people are not themselves equal in skills, work, education, and benefits of the society.

Again, here is one of these problems where you are "damned if you do and damned if you don't." Very frankly, yes, our constitution guarantees human freedom, but we have not been able to carry out all of our ideals. No country has. Some claim that active equal opportunity programs for minorities have, in effect, discriminated against the majority and limited their freedom and choice.

Also, we tend to judge other people by our own ideals rather than by our actual practice. Other countries often judge the United States by some of their ideals, not by their realities. I often point out the fact that, yes, we have a democratic constitution, and we have recently done a much better job in the court systems and in the equal opportunity commissions that have tried to enforce the terms of the constitution in their humane interpretation. But, we have a long way to go. The constitution is democratic, but its interpretation and implementation involve a constant fight to preserve human rights and the vitality of the democratic system. Freedom is never free. Its price must be paid. However, even with its flaws, American freedom still is a powerful magnet that promises dignity and opportunity and attracts thousands to its shores.

QUESTION 28

Is your law humane when you still have capital punishment?

RESPONSE

Actually, this has long been debated in legal and humanitarian circles in the United States. In the last several years, there have been four or five executions. In most of these cases the prisoners would not appeal their sentence, in a sense saying "go ahead with the execution, I do not want to live in prison."

However, we now have a number of cases where the laws in many states are now being appealed on various grounds. There are, I understand, over 600 people convicted of capital offenses sitting on "death row" awaiting execution. So, in effect, capital punishment is rarely carried out even in states where it is legal.

There is rising public reaction to increased violence and crime. But, just recently, a conference of Catholic bishops has come out with a pronouncement against capital punishment. I would say that we probably are not going to see a major reinstituting of capital punishment. If it does come back, it will only be in one or two states where the state laws and the state courts have again permitted it and where it has been judged not to be inordinate punishment for the crimes that have been committed.

QUESTION 29

You Americans say you are against socialism. What is so wrong with socialism? We cannot afford your wasteful ways. We just do not have the resources.

RESPONSE

My response to this is that I do not know what is wrong with socialism in every case. It might be ideal for you if your people are trained and conscientious and can make the socialist system work. I know what socialism is in terms of my personal observations of the Soviet Union, Poland, Czechoslavakia or Cuba. When I see the way those societies operate economically and socially, I see no comparison in terms of the productivity and social welfare of the United States. A totally government planned economy cuts incentives and rewards for innovation, hard work, and individualistic expression. It can be extremely effective, however, in mobilizing people in newly modernizing society for rapid change.

In the United States we have assumed some of the characteristics of social planning at both the state and federal levels. The government is much more active and involved in people's lives than it was even in my youth. In that sense we are more socialistic. In today's complex, interdependent society more of our economy and life is in the public sector in contrast to the private sector fifty years ago.

I am personally for a mixed economy, no matter what label you put on it. Socialism may be the thing at your stage of development that is most constructive for you. However, some of us have very real problems with some forms of socialism, especially those forms of Marxism, Leninism and Communism that advocate violent change and class warfare against the market economy system. We see totalitarianism as a threat to the kind of democratic world system we see as essential for our continued freedom and prosperity. It is very inefficient in terms of managing the material and nonmaterial, economic and social welfare of the nation.

What is wrong with socialism? It depends on the country. In some places there is probably nothing wrong in terms of what alternatives are available. Labels are very dangerous, but in general terms I want the most humane, efficient, and productive system for my country. In comparing the other systems of the world during my career, I have come to the conclusion that a mixed economy with a private sector and a public sector seems the most helpful.

Private enterprise systems of the market economies are often identified as wasteful because they produce so much. They do produce much waste in terms of the experience and resources of poor countries. Certainly, poor countries do not have the resources to spend on many of the competitive institutions, the social services, luxuries, or the private and volunteer services that you find in rich countries.

Certainly the kind of mixed economy in the United States may not be appropriate for a developing country. However, the concepts, ideas, and economic patterns are something that can be taken, adopted, and adapted, particularly in a cooperative fashion in an interdependent world society. You can get a blend that produces productivity and a large degree of freedom, independence, and national development without outside interference.

QUESTION 30

In Europe, we have quite a bit of difficulty in collecting taxes. How do you get people to pay?
RESPONSE

In many countries, particularly if the government is not very effective, it is difficult to get people to pay taxes. The rich often find ways of dodging taxes. Incidently this is also a problem in the United States that recent tax bills are seeking to correct.

One way in which tax collection was improved in the United States was when the Constitution was changed to permit federal income taxes.

Since then a tax on wage earners is usually deducted as the salary is earned. People pay taxes directly to the government; that is, the employer pays taxes directly to the government on the wage earner's salary. People who are self-employed have an obligation to pay taxes in quarterly installments based on estimated income. But, often they have lawyers who are skilled in finding what we call "loopholes," or exceptional rules in the tax laws that help them to avoid paying high taxes. People with considerable money often find ways to use such laws to avoid paying taxes.

For instance, homeowners have certain advantages over those who are renting. They can deduct the interest they pay on a mortgage from their incomes. They do not have to pay tax on that money. The person who is paying rent is not able to deduct part of his or her housing expense.

Another way of getting people to pay their taxes is to carefully monitor things like the dividends that are paid by corporations. Corporations must report the payment of that dividend, so if the government sees that the company has paid it to a person, but the person does not report it as income, the government can say "You have not paid your tax on that," and move to collect.

The government has developed rather sophisticated ways of checking how much money people are making. Still, there are various ways people are constantly trying to avoid and minimize their taxes. It is almost a contest between the government's ability to collect the taxes and find ways to prevent people from cheating, underreporting, or underpaying, and the people's constant attempt, both legally and illegally, to avoid paying taxes.

Excise taxes and sales taxes are often paid on products or services at the time that the service or the product is purchased, so the government gets an immediate collection. Another tax that is collected rather efficiently is the property tax. This is the tax people pay on their property and is used to provide for various services in the community. The United States probably has been more effective than most countries, but in Congress there is always a constant fight to pass laws that will force people and corporations with much money (who find ways to avoid paying taxes) to pay their fair share.

The United States government traditionally has been rather successful in preserving the image that it is the servant of all people and that it is not run by special interest groups. I think there is a general feeling on the part of the citizens that they have the duty and obligation as citizens to pay their taxes. I do think that, in a sense, it helps them control the government. They usually are critical of the waste in government, but they see the government as legitimate. They, as citizens, generally feel an obligation to support the community and the things for which their taxes are spent.

QUESTION 31
Wasn't President Kennedy's assassination part of a conspiracy of your far right (or far left), both to remove your progressive president and to increase international tension? Isn't Ted Kennedy in danger today?
RESPONSE

The assassination of President Kennedy had a stunning impact on Americans. Virtually all adults remember where they were on the 23rd of November in 1963, when he was assassinated. I remember that I was going to work with a Peace Corps group at Columbia Teachers College. The whole university was shut down, in shock and mourning. Since then there have been many controversies in the United States and around the world about Kennedy's assassination and the assassination of Oswald, the man that was accused of shooting him.

It was sort of a fantastic thing. Oswald had been a marine, gone to the Soviet Union, married a Soviet wife, and gotten mixed up in all kinds of organizations. That a man like this could undertake an assassination of a U.S. President was an amazing event that just stupified people.

One logic says: It is impossible that one man could engineer, manipulate and conceive of a thing like this without any help or without any additional purpose. On the other hand, we have had quite a few presidents—Lincoln, McKinley and others—who have either been shot or attacked by people in our diversified, individualistic society. Some maniacs just "blow their tops" and take this upon themselves as an individual act. There is no absolute security against this kind of spontaneous violence.

With the increase of terrorism, there is the mounting feeling that there exists a conspiracy that is either of the right or of the left. I have heard many people say that Kennedy was killed by a communist inspired plot and not by superconservatives or militant anti-communists who wanted to get rid of him. As recently as 1980, people were still investigating and trying to exhume Oswald's body, to bring it up for research and investigation. They were trying to prove that Oswald was not Oswald, but some Soviet spy that had been "planted" to kill Kennedy.

There is still controversy, even though the best juridical and legal people of the time have made the determination that President Kennedy was killed by one man in an individual enterprise, one who was demented and enraged. The controversy, the mythology, and the books will continue for ages because of the literary symbolism and the seemingly conflicting evidence reported in such books.

Americans still ask questions, but I think that they are fairly satisfied with the notion that the President was killed by Oswald in an individual act and not as part of a conspiracy. Nevertheless, I have lived through so many things in history where past facts come up ten to fifteen, a hundred years later that seem to change the basic interpretation of what has happened. This could happen with the Kennedy case.

All public figures are in danger today, be they private or political, when terrorism is used as a political tool. Paradoxically, security is more demanding in an open, individualistic society than in closed, authoritarian countries. Senator Kennedy is certainly a public figure

Section III:
Americans in the World Economy

Whereas security issues based on political and military foundations dominate East-West relations, political and economic concerns dominate conflicts in North-South relations. And, increasingly the agenda for debate and consideration confronting all nations of the world has been expanded to include questions of economics and development.

As we consider commonly asked questions concerning economic dealings of United States' firms with other countries, as well as the economic policies of the American government in the world, we would do well to recognize the likely standard context of our questioner. It is imperative that we also consciously restrain our defensive mechanisms when questions are critical of our economic system or of how we act in the world economy. While we may be justified in the defense we might offer, we can be assured that it will do little to change the questioner's point of view. Rather, we need to try to understand his position, respect his right to believe as he does, and then try to give a balanced response. We might do well to shift the preferred goal of our communication with that questioner from one of defense to that of offering a fair and well-reasoned answer that is sensitive to his perspective while not necessarily giving in to it.

While risking excessive generalization, we would do well to broadly characterize a perception widely shared among the less advanced market economies, or what are often termed the underdeveloped countries. That general perception can perhaps be summarized as follows: "Our underdevelopment is not solely a function of our inability to adapt the technologies and production practices of the advanced industrial economies to our needs. We are not underdeveloped for want of frequent interchange and cooperation with the advanced countries of the world. Rather, we are underdeveloped because of, not inspite of, a long enduring relationship with the major economic actors in the world economy. The nature of that relationship is markedly uneven and disadvantageous to us and beneficial to you. We have contributed much to your economic advance by providing cheap resources and open markets for your manufactured products. The result has been that we have remained poor and you have enjoyed rapid economic advantage."

Now, we would be sorely mistaken if we were to suppose that such sentiments are felt by only a few. We would be similarly wrong if we were to credit such declarations to only the most radical elements of the societies with which we interact. And, we would be foolishly narrow-minded if we were to characterize such perceptions as only the creations of communist propaganda widely propagated and believed in the Third World. No, these are perceptions born of national experience over long centuries of relations with first colonial empires and then economically advanced nations. We need not consider such statements as unfounded expressions of anti-imperialist slogans. These are the products of first-hand experience and a growing awareness that the situation of the people in these less advanced societies is conditioned by happenings in the world economy, and that their national governments have been relatively unable to avoid the negative consequences of such tight integration in the world economic system.

Let us briefly review some of the historical grounds upon which these perceptions have been founded. In so doing, we first need to remember that it matters little whether the basis for the perceptions often held by those asking us questions are or are not supported by hard evidence. These attitudes are nevertheless firmly held. At best we can incorporate in our response expressions which might entice our reader to consider another side of the story.

Whether we label free trade as a form of imperialism or not, it is not difficult to see why people in less developed countries readily identify with some of the inequities of trade. Consider just the question of removing tariffs and quotas that inhibit trade. To universally remove barriers to trade would be to bring uneven benefits to the trading nations. If a nation such as the United States has numerous and diverse goods to trade, while another nation (such as most less advanced market economies) has relatively fewer goods to trade, then it is little wonder that increasing the "freedom" of trade benefits the former nation while not equally benefiting, or even harming, the other. With obstacles to trade eliminated, the less advanced market economy will buy goods on the international market and will postpone development of that industry within its own national market. And, as the less advanced market economy comes to regularly consume that imported product, it will likely continue imports even if prices increase. Dependence on foreign sources for such goods increases to the disadvantage of the less advanced market economy. Foreign trade with the advanced market economies brings relative disadvantages for the less advanced market economies.

Also, consider the response of the less advanced market economies to penetration of their national economies by transnational corporations. As large foreign firms directly invest in these countries, local firms are often displaced. Since the technology employed by these large firms often eliminates the need to hire workers, expectations for job creation are often held in vain. Moreover, as these transnational corporations come to dominate certain sectors of a national economy, there is little that local entrepreneurs can do to guide these economic activities for their own national development. Increasingly large shares of the production of transnational corporations are also exported, reducing the positive side-effects of increased production introduced via the transnational corporations. It could be argued that in the absence of such expanded markets that trade provides, or without the direct investment of transnational corporations, economic growth in these less advanced market economies would not increase as rapidly as it might. Indeed, many countries literally clamour for the investment of capital brought by transnational corporations or available from foreign banks. However, as these people become more and more sophisticated economically, they fully realize that those relationships are relatively more advantageous to the transnational corporations and to their countries of origin than to themselves. Consequently, an anti-foreign business or even anti-American speech becomes quite useful in pursuing individual business or even national interests. And, those groups that find themselves on the short end of the economic distribution evident in their countries are often led to strongly argue such a case.

At least we should recognize the perception that economic dealings with the United States and other advanced market economies are not equally beneficial. Indeed, over time a given nation may become relatively worse off, although not absolutely disadvantaged. Finally, it should be pointed out that vigorously promoting this type of perception can have benefits for governments and specific interest groups. In effect, highlighting the negative effects of dealings with the United States and transnational corporations serves to de-emphasize the internal problems confronting a society, and which the government seems relatively unable to resolve. Economic failures of governmental programs or of local firms can be blamed on the international market and on problems associated with American foreign aid programs, direct foreign investments via transnational corporations, and foreign loans which lead to heavy indebtedness and high costs of servicing that indebtedness.

It should be re-emphasized that little is to be gained by challenging the accuracy of such claims. If our presentation of these specific perceptions leads to such an endeavor, then the purpose of this volume has been defeated. Rather, our purpose has been to illustrate the basis for a widely shared set of perceptions that likely condition the way questioners ask their questions and the way they expect you to respond. Your intent is not to defend your position by a frontal assault, but should rather be to lessen tension by recognizing your questioner may have a valid point, and by then indicating a possible way of seeing the issue in what to him is a "new light."

With this as background, the questions to which Dr. Vetter offers useful responses take on greater meaning. While it sometimes may appear that he could have offered a stronger response, in the sense of more vigorously defending the position of the United States or of its internationally operative programs, firms, or citizens, he chooses not to so engage his questioners. He usefully recognizes the perceptions of his questioners, expresses sensitivity to their position, and then leads them to recognize that the issue at hand is not quite as "black and white" as implied by the tone and content of the question that has been asked.

Why doesn't the United States support the Third World and its efforts for a New Economic Order?

RESPONSE

Seeking greater economic justice and opportunity, many of the Third World Countries are demanding a New Economic Order in the United Nations organizations and Organizations of Non-Alligned States. The United States hears this appeal. It recognizes the fact a new order is already with us.

The United States has participated in helping millions of people directly and indirectly by providing health care, credit and technical assistance. The standard of living in the world has risen remarkably in the past couple of decades. Yet, bringing the developing countries into parity with countries that have had three centuries of industrial experience remains elusive. There has been a measurable increase in interchange between the Third World and industrialized countries. There has been a closing of the gap in some areas. However, sometimes due to the lack of ability to utilize and absorb capital and technology in some under-developed countries, the overall gap has broadened.

Recently certain Third World countries have improved their position in the world economy. Clearly, this has been the case for oil exporting countries like Nigeria, Saudi Arabia, Mexico, Venezuela, Kuwait, and others. Advances by newly industrializing countries such as Brazil, Taiwan, South Korea, Hong Kong, and Singapore have also been impressive.

Nevertheless, closing the gap culturally, economically, politically and educationally has been and undoubtedly will continue to be a long process. To say that the United States does not support such change is erroneous. The United States invests billions of dollars in international enterprises. However, in proportion to the United States GNP, there is a lot more that we could do. This is a question of political and financial adjustment. More funds have to come from the private sector as well as from government. This may be done through bilateral or multilateral contract or agreement. Additional activities have to be done in cooperation with other nations through the medium of the United Nations, non-profit organizations, corporations, and governments.

The appropriateness of particular adjustments in the world economy is hotly contested. The tensions that we see in the United Nations and other international organizations, such as the World Bank and the International Monetary Fund, have become acute. Developing an infrastructure, promoting capital accumulation and trade, transferring technology, advancing labor skills and health, and properly using resources are now world problems. They are receiving emphasis by an increasingly complex network of organizations, institutions, political leaders and vested interests.

Every responsible leader that I have spoken to has stated that, in the United States, concerns are no longer exclusively in the realm of East-West relations. North-South relationships are expanding. Every country in the world has potential to influence every other country in this increasingly interdependent world. The fact is that the United States is not as relatively powerful in the world as it used to be. More than ever before, practical development programs have to be implemented in a cooperative manner.

The question of what is just and unjust is something that people are striving to define. It remains one of the great challenges for the world to answer. Growing interdependence requires that we find an equitable arrangement among all nations. One indication of new economic orders and patterns to come might be seen in the case of the great financial success of the American films, "Star Wars" and "E.T." around the world. The success has created a market for dolls and toys based on the movie characters. But this toy business will not create jobs in America because the toys are actually being made in Taiwan, Korea, and the Philippines.

As economies of the developed countries shift from industry to information and service, capital intensive industry is shifting jobs and power to the Third World.

QUESTION 33

Why do you let your businessmen get rich on our country's wealth by exploiting our natural resources and then selling over-priced American goods to us? And why do you claim that you are helping our people when your aid only makes the rich richer and does not help our poor people?

RESPONSE

It seems to be a basic belief that the industrial countries, such as the United States, are taking advantage of developing countries by taking their resources. We acknowledge that even now as in the past there has been exploitation. There have been some opportunistic people in international trade and commerce. We would hope that you would not judge all by the past actions of self-appointed opportunists. Many who were considered imperialists or exploiters in the past really were not accepted in their own country.

There were also pioneers who brought important change but operated under different international morality and saw nothing wrong in taking advantage of weaker, less experienced people. They were operating in activities for which there was little precedent. By today's standard they did exploit, but it was not a time of international standards and controls.

Today in almost every country there are local people who are responsible for exploiting their own poor, and they may be involved with similar people from other countries. Ideally, if governments were honest and could protect the interest of their people, see that fair taxes were levied and collected, and assure that all the people, foreign and national, would obey the laws of the land, then expanding exploitation of humans would be checked.

It would be unrealistic to suppose that there has not been a great deal of social and economic injustice in the world. There are those who are constantly leveling the charge of "imperialism" at the United States. While occasionally valid in part, this generalization is unwarranted. There are many instances in which the United States has helped develop excellent programs for the benefit of other nations' development of institutions and management that will help them protect themselves and effectively work in world markets. The American Congress has mandated that U.S. official AID programs must concentrate on the poorest sectors in developing countries to aid more balanced growth. There is a law in the United States that prohibits corporations from bribing representatives of foreign governments to obtain working contracts with their countries. Violators are prosecuted. In the huge trillion dollar world market, business must be increasingly fair, honest, and accountable to prosper.

QUESTION 34

The decisions of multinational corporations affect the lives of millions, yet who knows how they are operated? Who really runs ITT? Are the multinationals neo-imperialist organizations fronting for U.S. business interests?

RESPONSE

Multinational corporations can be Japanese—like Mitsubishi, Sony or Hitachi; Dutch—like KLM; German, French, American or Swiss. There is no doubt that their power, capital, organizations and resources cross national boundaries.

In the past these people have tried to expand their profits and take advantage of weakness in many areas of the world. Where countries did not have control of their own bureaucracies to the extent that they could make these companies obey the laws or make them accountable for taxes and responsible operations, there have been great abuses. The payment of bribes to get contracts and the use of financial power and commercial intelligence have been employed to take advantage of weaker countries or weaker people.

On the other hand, multinational organizations have contributed to the exchange of technology and the commencement of capital accumulation that can develop human resources in the world economy. Since 1950 trade has increased from about sixty billion dollars to over two trillion dollars for all the countries in the world. In part, this has been made possible through the impressive efficiency and ability of these large corporate entities to appropriately work across national time and cultural boundaries.

There have been abuses by people and organizations, but their contributions to world economic growth have been tremendous. And, over the years increasing accountability of these organizations has been noted. One of the most effective tools against abuse has been an investigative world press.

It is interesting that large foreign corporations based in other countries have for some time been entering the United States' economy by purchasing American companies. They are producing jobs in the United States often with higher productivity than American companies. Some Japanese companies now operate very large plants in the United States. We do not consider this Japanese imperialism because these companies are obeying the laws of the United States, paying proper taxes, and obeying all important rules of world commerce.

As for who runs ITT? Probably a group of managers who are under consistent pressure from governments, stockholders and corporate interests in the many countries where ITT operates. ITT is dependent upon government cooperation, regulation and permission in many fields that determine whether they make a profit or not. Governments in many countries regulate their activities, as is done in the United States.

In many cases one finds that a government's interests and the multinational corporation's interests are in conflict. Often these conflicts are not publicized, leading people to talk as if these corporations were an instrumentality of the American government. There is a real division of power in the United States between the private sector and the public sector. They are often in competition. Critics of the system often paint the picture as if these big companies and the government were in constant collusion or cooperation. This is just not the case, as we have seen in the example of government objection to American companies participating in the construction of the Soviet natural gas pipeline in Europe. American businessmen have often suffered in competition with European and Japanese companies that have much greater government support and protection.

QUESTION 35
Why is it that aid programs such as those in Latin America and Africa do not work? Are these just ploys to make us dependent on the Yankees?
RESPONSE

The United States receives a variety of requests to set up development programs. This has been the case for many years. One example can be seen with the reconstruction programs after World War II. This was tremendously effective in the rebuilding of Europe. The actual construction was done by Europeans using their skills and technology, while America furnished consultants, capital, and planning.

When America goes into many of the Third World countries who desire assistance, we are not actually reconstructing an economy. Rather, we are trying to set up a workable economic base for the capital accumulation necessary to establish a foundation for new industry and agricultural reform. However, in the final analysis, any outside assistance can only be of marginal help.

There undoubtedly is some truth to the claim that many of the assistance programs have also benefitted American organizations, companies and industries. Many American firms in the private sector have actually worked on government programs (on contract either to the American government or to other governments) that were receiving financial assistance from the Alliance for Progress or the Agency for International Development. Although some abuses have occurred, the majority of projects have been honest, and with added experience, education, research, and resources, it will be increasingly effective for their nations.

In a certain sense, these assistance programs have become engines of change which have developed new potentials, opened up new organizational institutions, and given educational, technical, and specialized training to thousands and thousands of people. On the other hand, many thought economic assistance programs would produce political stability. What has actually happened in some cases has caused changes in thinking on both sides. Sometimes these programs have only produced new elite groups. Some people have prostituted their educational skills and experiences to get power to wield over their people.

The Alliance for Progress did not really meet the expectations of either the Latin American countries or the Americans who planned it. This is generally true with innovative projects. These programs have caused tremendous changes in attitudes, resources and opportunities in many countries. People themselves have been changed by the communication and technological revolutions. While temporarily unsettling, these changes are certainly on the positive side of progress. Good seeds have been planted and more and more the harvest is forthcoming.

Perhaps we all need to recognize the magnitude of obstacles obstructing fruition of aid program goals. The gap between developed, industrialized countries and the underdeveloped, non-industrialized countries is tremendous. It is a great challenge to work out an equitable, hopeful system of relief in our global community.

QUESTION 36

Americans have been in our country for so long; you make promises and expect us to follow your directions. Do you think you can buy our friendship with these assistance programs?
RESPONSE

In the past many of our programs, particularly military assistance, were considered programs to which strings were attached. Americans thought that because they were conducting assistance programs the recipients should be grateful to them and that they had an obligation to be friendly, loyal, supportive, and "to fall in line." Americans felt, in effect, "Here, we're using taxpayer's money, our resources, and we do everything we can to help these other people and look at how ungrateful they are. Why can't they support us in the United Nations? Why can't they quit being critical of us?"

There have been misunderstandings. Many American assistance programs have been for mutual purposes. Of course, many of these programs have been carried out by American organizations that have made a profit for themselves. We have sent American specialists and supervisors and paid their salaries when they were consultants in other countries, but then charged the fees back to the countries in which they were consulting. So, there is some legitimate criticism and feeling that the United States demands friendship, gratitude, discipline, and support for giving assistance which is actually helping us as much as it is helping the recipient.

At the same time this has caused the recipient to pile up large debts that have to be serviced, often for things that are not too valuable to their country. I think there has been some very conscious consideration of this in forming new assistance legislation, and in developing new assistance programs. I think it takes a complete look at a specific country, its needs and conditions, to reduce these problems. It takes hard questioning, yielding specific answers. And, where it is appropriate, it is important to admit shortcoming, to say we are sorry to see such problems. Then we need to demonstrate some of the things that have been done to correct them, either by the local government or by the American government.

However, the fact that the great majority of these binational economic and military relationships continue after 30 years of change seems to indicate that they are, in fact, reciprocal and of mutual benefit.

QUESTION 37

Many of us believe that capitalism is inhumane. Isn't socialism much more "Christian" than capitalism, much more humane, much more promoting of the welfare and love and friendship among people in different classes, among different kinds of people? Your capitalism is inhumane, just look at what is happening in your country: the crime, the violence, and the racism.

RESPONSE

When I hear a question like this, I often ask myself, or ask the other person, what "capitalism" are you talking about? Throughout history there have been some countries working under a capitalist system that has been just horrible.

Actually, capitalism in the United States is a mixed system. It is partly a governmental-public sector, which is the emphasis for the socialists. In some ways, a country like India, that calls itself socialist, has more of its economy in the private sector than does the United States. American capitalism today has been greatly reformed because of the pressure and power of the people. Significant redistribution of wealth and power has occurred to a much broader segment of the population than was the case in my grandfather's time.

On the other hand, there is very little ideological difference between the Christian socialist or the democratic socialist in European countries, the United States and other market economy countries. Each is a mixed economy—public and private. Each poses quite a contrast to the stereotype of the racist, monopolistic, imperialistic capitalist of the olden days.

As far as it being more Christian, I do not know. I have seen some Christian governments that have been absolute dictatorships. I can remember Franco's Spain which was highly Christian but very fascistic and dictatorial. I think that the best principles of Christianity, socialism, pluralistic democracy (as it is practiced in the United States), and communism are very humanistic; they all advocate ideal societies in their pronouncements. The question is, though, how does each system for organization of human events come out when these different systems are put into effect?

I think I have seen good and bad communist systems; I have seen good and bad capitalist or democratic systems. I think that it is very dangerous to talk about these things in general terms. I am personally convinced that we have made tremendous progress in the United States in reforming traditional capitalism and making it much more humanistic and viable in terms of a just, productive, and peaceful society.

In my life I have seen the American population more than double to over 230 million people. Most things have increased, including crime, but I see a more humane, just, productive life for the masses. In purely socialist countries, I have not seen the productivity to make that kind of uplift possible.

QUESTION 38

Isn't your use of energy, of oversized cars and endless appliances selfish and irresponsible? If the world oil supply falls short, those of us in smaller countries will suffer. You have the power to get what you need. Besides, your shortages have driven prices up causing inflation and endangering our economy.

RESPONSE

It is certainly understandable how people in other countries could see America's consumption of energy as both irresponsible and selfish. Much of the American economic and social culture has been built over the last fifty years on the assumption that energy was both easy to get and cheap, not only for the United States, but for the whole world.

As a matter of fact, the world energy shortage is a relatively new thing. Until about ten years ago, the United States was actually exporting oil. So, we are in the process of a very difficult change, reflected in the changing of our automobile manufacturers, insulation of our houses, and construction changes.

Of course, this is being speeded by the problems of inflation and other financial and monetary problems, where energy is so much more expensive. Citizens of the United States are taking individual and collective steps to change this very serious situation. So are we "selfish and irresponsible"? Possibly in appearance, but I think that in this time of inflation and increasing shortages the American public and the American government are trying hard to respond to this problem by changing energy use patterns at home and working out cooperative programs for trade and emergencies with other countries.

78

QUESTION 39

Why is there an American energy crisis? Doesn't this indicate bad planning and waste, and perhaps dishonesty in your big oil companies?
RESPONSE

In a world with multiple energy requirements, there naturally needs to be a retrenchment to evaluate how much has to go how far. The questions beg to be answered by people both friendly and hostile to American interests and activities. "Energy" has become one of those internationally emotional words. Twenty-five years ago it was simply a noun. Now it is a household word symbolizing an unbelievably complicated problem.

Why is there an energy crisis? There are political implications rooted in the conflicts in the Middle East countries. Each is fighting for territory, power, survival or all three. The United States is seeking to help Arab nations realize their political interests and assist Israel in remaining an independent nation.

The energy crisis, however, goes far beyond this. Growing industrialization has dramatically increased the consumption of oil, which in turn has intensified the crisis. Today more countries are making energy consuming products. Hence, the market for and use of energy has increased phenomenally. The needs of people living here in a culture that was developed on the basis of cheap energy are making some expensive and frustrating adjustments, as are the suppliers and producers. Be they from the OPEC nations or the large oil companies, people with 'energy power' have also had economic problems that have shown limits of their power. International negotiation, energy research and conservation, and practical changes of energy users are attacking many aspects of the energy crisis.

For example, in times past it was not economical to spend more money to insulate houses when energy to heat them was minimal in cost. Now that energy costs have risen dramatically it is necessary to recondition poorly insulated homes. Big cars were made in America because people living in a country with great open spaces to travel wanted safety, speed and comfort. Highways and road systems were built on the assumption that gasoline would always be relatively cheap. Now there has had to be a radical change in the design of automobiles. These things have made a significant impact on the American economy and society.

Another situation also exists where socio-economic considerations have been affected by the energy crisis. In the northeast part of the United States where there is bitter cold weather, people are having a very difficult time because many of the big industries are moving to the "sun belt" in the South to save money and energy. The cold climate has been too costly. This has produced some real tensions in the economic structure of the nation.

The energy crisis is difficult to solve because of the many and varied needs of oil companies, the American public, Congress, the President, and the OPEC nations. It is not only our national problem but an international challenge.

QUESTION 40

How can you have poverty and unemployment in your country when you are so rich? How can you have poverty in the midst of so much skill, science, technology, resources, and education?

RESPONSE

There has been a tremendous change in the standard of living for the people of this country. Yet, progress and change have not been equal. There is poverty in the United States, although it is often comparative poverty. This state of comparative poverty is generally found in ghettoized segments of our large cities such as New York, Washington, Chicago, and Los Angeles. There are large concentrations of low-income blacks, Hispanics, whites, and other ethnic groups. Often, however, you will find homes in these areas equipped with refrigerators, freezers, and televisions. People often have their own automobiles and other items which are indicators of wealth in Latin America, Africa, and Asia. Poverty does exist in the United States, but it is more relative than absolute. Government and private welfare systems insure basic necessities for all citizens.

Over the last fifty years the basic shape of the United States profile has changed. You still have people who are very wealthy. Presently, the shape of the income distribution appears like that of an egg. Most Americans are in the middle class. Still, there are people who are relatively poor. That is one of the real challenges confronting the American society. Poverty is a reality, and it is something that involves much more than money. There is in effect a culture of poverty involving values, attitudes, laws, resources, and institutions. In the 1960's President Johnson declared a 'War on Poverty' that brought programs that made significant progress. Other programs helped but cost more than the nation could afford. We are constantly trying to balance needs and resources. Poverty might be eliminated in a wealthy person society, but in a generally free American society great variety continues to exist in the economic life. Poverty continues in the midst of abundance for the majority.

Section IV:
American Foreign Policy

We are now approaching the half century landmark of being one of the world's major powers. For much of that time we have been the dominant world power. Such status brings both good fortunes economically and politically, as well as criticism from any number of sources for any number of divergent reasons.

Leadership has not been a responsibility from which we have or perhaps could have resigned. Many still look to us for advice, economic assistance, technological transfers, and political-military security. Others are significantly more concerned that we might exercise our strength in such a way as to interfere with their pursuit of national interests. Others are fearful of the potential consequences of America's seeming decline in power in the world.

Whatever the particular perspective of those who may ask questions concerning America's role in world affairs, we can be certain that they perceive their lives and the history of their country as having been some-how affected by American foreign policy or by the behaviors of Ameri-ca's internationally visible firms, organizations, and citizens. We may venture to convince our questioner that such pervasive influence has not been the explicit intent of the United States, but that in no way will less-en the perceived impact of that influence. We cannot escape responsi-bility for affecting others; we cannot deny our political history as a world power.

Perhaps we may be tempted to justify our actions in world affairs on the basis of wholesome, right, humane, and beneficient intent. We might even be tempted to argue that the track record of our performance as a responsible world citizen is largely above reproach. Yet, whether well in-tended or not, or whether the negative outcomes of our policies and be-haviors have all been unpredictable and unexpected or not, it is no less the case that over the course of our history, as a world power, some na-tions and some people have perceived their interests to have been im-pacted negatively by our actions. To expect history to record otherwise would be folly.

Consequently, it behooves persons that are engaged in frequent inter-national interchange to become well acquainted with international af-fairs from a global perspective. Ours is not the only interpretation of the role of the United States as a major world power. Other analyses of that role are forthcoming from journalists and the media throughout the world. We can ill afford to be ignorant of those alternative views of America's international politics. Local accounts of that role may at times excite an angry or defensive reaction on our part, requiring us to remem-ber that whether valid or not, such perceptions may well be broadly shared. Moreover, in any case, such negative perceptions surely have some grounding in the past experience of that journalist or of a fairly large portion of a given society.

We might even do well to recognize certain distinct blemishes on our record as a world power. Surely we are not infallible; our judgment is not always prophetic and sound. And, admitting to such mistakes does not necessarily detract from assertions of the overall soundness of our world leadership. At the same time, it should be readily apparent that excessive criticism of other world powers, particularly blatant denunciations of their political culture and ideologies, will bring us little mileage in an at-tempt to develop a relationship with a particular foreign citizen or or-ganization.

Perhaps now, more than at any other period of world history, one can suggest that we see signs of a "world society" emerging. This world society may even be becoming something more than an early intermixing of largely nation-centered societies. And, in our dealings with people throughout the globe we may well find it advantageous to promote this perception of a world society. Surely our world is today more economically interdependent than during any previous historical period. And, while such interdependence, such frequent economic interchange the world over, may open the door to positive social, cultural and political interchange, it may under certain conditions be the forerunner of world conflicts. It is surely the case in these times of economic interdependence that if we doggedly adhere to political, cultural, and social "nationalism," this interdependence bodes more ill than good.

The intent of this discussion is not to suggest that Americans traveling the globe in whatever capacity must be apologetic when the United States' role in world affairs is discussed. We have not been an empire builder; we have not sought to rule the world nor any set of nations in the world. It is precisely because we have not been interested in expanding our territory and sovereign influence that our attempts at promoting interdependence, politically and socially as well as economically, may be perceived as credible. However, no longer can we suppose, if we ever did, that the countries of the world owe allegiance to the United States. We cannot expect nations to submit to American leadership as many once did in the past. We can perhaps foster the worldview that the United States and its citizens wish to perform a constructive role in our increasingly interdependent world.

One final point needs mentioning. You may take exception to some of the answers offered by Dr. Vetter in this section. At the same time, the answers are sufficiently rich in substance that they may help you formulate your preferred answer. You may also feel inclined to cite different historical materials or to offer somewhat different interpretations. Such is your prerogative, and neither we nor Dr. Vetter mean to suggest that all of the "true" answers are provided here. We know, and surely you know by now, that such is not the case.

Nevertheless, we would again commend to you the "style" or "format" of Dr. Vetter's responses. While not agreeing entirely with the tone of given questions, and while at times forthrightly stating his views of the rightness or at least understandability of American actions, he does not belittle the implicit insights of the questioner. Also, he does not overly attempt to justify past actions, although he does try to explain many of them. Rather, he attempts to communicate America's desire for positive citizenship in the world community. He emphasizes our recognition that the world is different now from that of the immediate post-World War II period, and that interdependence is here to stay. In the context of that interdependence, Dr. Vetter suggests that the United States has the desire to make meaningful contributions.

QUESTION 41

Does the United States really want disarmament? What would your monopolists and military men do if you really disarmed?

RESPONSE

This is a question that is asked frequently even here in the United States. What about the "merchants of death" and "the militarists and the hawks and the hardliners?" There are probably counterparts to these in Europe, Japan, and the Soviet Union. I think this is a very difficult question.

Of course the United States, in theory, wants disarmament, but in reality, it is unlikely. The military in most countries is seen as the most realistic insurance policy for peace. It is thought to be analogous to a fire department or a police department in a world where there is much unbridled and uncontrolled violence.

We saw the greatest military fabricating system in the world established by the United States during World War II. After that war, disarmament came quite easily and quickly once there was security enough for real disarmament. There was world-wide disarmament at the end of the Second World War, although many people predicted that a depression would result in America. But, there was much rebuilding to do.

Just look at the conditions of the world today. See the tremendous human needs and potential markets and outlets for creative and productive services. There is plenty for the "monopolists," and the industrial and commercial economic forces to do other than to be involved in armaments, which is basically a non-productive use of capital.

On the other hand, I think we must also realize that military forces in many countries are part of the governmental structure. Also, they are often a valuable source for training and disciplining people. Paradoxically, in many countries of Latin America the military is a main elevator for career and social mobility. In many cases it is where people go to get an education, learn the ways of the world, and learn administration and management skills. This type of knowledge is often used in politics, economics, and social action.

Of course, everybody would like to see universal, general world disarmament, as the Soviets have so often urged in their appeals. We also want that. But, given the realities of life, unfortunately, such action is unlikely. People and the resources of industry are dedicated to defense or to deterring the use of force.

QUESTION 42

Are you really sincere about détente? Why do you spend so much money on arms and sell so many arms to other people, even to our country? Why do you export all these arms? Do you really want peace? Do you really want détente?

RESPONSE

In American foreign policy during each administration since World War II, people have realized that there is no alternative, particularly among the superpowers, to some kind of détente or some alternative for settling differences by force.

In this nuclear age I think there is recognition by leaders in all powerful countries that there must be movement towards peace, although there are often great disagreements. However, détente has slightly different connotations in the United States and the Soviet Union. Détente, in the context of "peaceful co-existence," as the Soviets would say, exists when countries of different economic and social systems can selectively work together while avoiding intervention in the internal affairs of other nations, but this does not imply lessening of class warfare or conflict between different ideological systems.

Détente, as initiated by the Nixon Administration, envisioned that many areas of interaction between the Soviet Union and the United States should be opened to move from confrontation to negotiations that could reconcile the hostilities between systems. Examples included: peaceful development of nuclear energy, the exploration of Antarctica, and cancer research. About sixteen different commissions were created. In addition, there was a burgeoning of trade between the two countries.

However, over time we have found that there were activities encouraged and supported by the Soviet Union that were undercutting American national interest for building a peaceful and pluralistic world society. We watched intervention by the Soviets, often with the cooperation of the Cubans, in armed conflicts in places like Angola, Ethiopia, and, of course, Afghanistan in December of 1979. This prompted active recollections of the appeasement experiences of Munich and the Rhineland in the 1930's that had failed to placate Hitler's demands. President Carter and his Administration decided that some definite things had to be done to show American disapproval of the use of force, aggression, and intervention by Soviet interests in other countries. President Carter linked

USA-USSR détente to Soviet responsible behavior in other parts of the world. Since then, there has been a delay in the development of détente in quite a few areas, not just with the cessation of American participation in the Olympics, but also in many areas of trade, cultural exchange, technology transfers, and the sale of agricultural goods. President Reagan has continued this "linkage," especially in regard to Central America, the Middle East and Poland.

Behind all this, of course, is the tremendous competition between the superpowers. One large component of the credibility and believability of the powers on each side, or on the several sides of world debate and competition, is armaments and military preparedness. In recent years, particularly during the American involvement in Vietnam, the Soviets have not only continued to modernize their conventional and nuclear military, but have, in the judgment of many people, gone beyond the requirements of defense into developments that can be used only for offensive purposes.

Of course, the great debate is how to keep parity, an equality of force, which in effect can be a form of détente for deterring the situation where one power or another gets predominant force, and where one or the other might be tempted to use such force to offset the power of other countries. Right now, this question of defense is a very important one in the interactions, negotiations, and psychological interface of these two very different systems. America and the Soviet Union have exported arms to allies and also to other people who have tried to sustain their regional security and stability within their own countries. Armament sales to places like Iran have been greatly criticized, although at the time they made a lot of sense in the context of alliances. The Shah of Iran was an ally of the Western powers and a sustainer of stability in that area of the world. There seemed to be justification in terms of national interest to supply arms. As for the wisdom of sustaining the Shah's administration, we are going to be debating that for a long, long time.

The sad fact is that as long as soverign national leaders feel armaments essential to their national security, and as long as there are competing arms suppliers anxious to supply arms to help their security industries and allies, international arms sales will continue.

There are increasing voices in America and in all countries demanding arms reduction and those voices are forcing world leaders to continue negotiations.

QUESTION 43
Why are your leaders arguing over the SALT Treaties and nuclear

freezes? Your NATO allies have agreed with the SALT Treaty, and yet you don't sign it yourself. Don't you want to stop the arms race?
RESPONSE

Here is an example of American executive and legislative powers not coming to an agreement over a treaty that was signed after seven years of negotiation between the Soviet Union and the United States. Even the present administration now disapproves of the SALT treaty. I think that one of the reasons that there has not been a ratification by the Senate is that there is a large group in the American legislature that does not believe that this treaty really limits arms. Theoretically, it puts a lid on the production of certain catagories of arms and would be the prelude to negotiating a third treaty that would actually begin to reduce arms. But opponents in the American legislature feel that the Soviets benefitted more from the terms of this treaty than did the United States. So, the opposition was able to stop President Carter's attempt to get ratification.

President Carter's approach, of course, was terminated by the November 1980 election. President Reagan views negotiations on strategic arms limitation as vital, and has already sent people representing his point of view to the Soviet Union. Negotiations have reopened in Geneva, continuing an effort to get not only a limitation on the building of armaments, but to also establish some concrete negotiations to reduce armaments.

This country and all countries, including the Soviet Union, are shouldering a tremendous burden in arms production. I think all sincere, realistic people see the expense of this, and are very frustrated that some workable agreement has not been worked out. The Soviets say that they do not want superiority, that they are working for mutual and equal security. Yet, many of the people evaluating the treaty feel that the treaty would allow increases in Soviet superiority in some key fields. So, this is a period of re-evaluation.

QUESTION 44

Why is the Soviet Union surpassing America in science and military power? Is it because their education system and discipline are better than yours?
RESPONSE

The Soviet Union is not necessarily passing us in science and military power, but there are areas where they appear to have passed us. In my visits to the Soviet Union, I have been impressed by certain things that I have seen. We have to always remember something about authoritarian or dictatorial societies, however, whether they are fascist, communist, monopolist, or whatever. If they have power, they have power to bring their best people and best resources into priority concerns. Where they give high priority to subsidize selective things, they are able to create recognizable excellence.

The museums of the world are full of examples of artistic and scientific excellence created in dictatorships, empires, czardoms, and monarchies, where the ruling powers brought their best people and resources to work on priorities. This has certainly happened in the Soviet Union where military development has been an area of priority. Another example is space research. The Soviets have drained many of their other areas of concentration to also put emphasis on sports as well as science and technology. They have succeeded with intelligent, bright people coming out of a long history of science, technology, and study which the Russian nation has had going for hundreds of years. People out of these traditions have produced real excellence in various areas.

A basic observation, however, is that few Russians have received Nobel prizes. Few people have seen an organized contribution to humanity. Happily, this is changing because many of their institutes, organizations, and universities are turning out well qualified people and excellent work in certain prioritized, subsidized areas.

Generally, however, it seems that the Soviet Union is coming to the West for the further development of science, high technology, and management. Some of their basic research is excellent. However, their supply system, in their bureaucratic system as well as management, is often extremely frustrating to scientists and technicians unless they work in priority areas. They do not get the goods they need, interchange with fellow scientists in other parts of the world, publications, computers, or the resources and freedom they need to continue in a sophisticated fashion.

They have made the military field a high priority and have produced some great technology. It is not necessarily because their educational system is better. Some of their system is excellent, and where they have put resources into priorities there have been some amazing performances.

On the general level though, the higher education system in American excels. In access, quality, across the board research, teaching, experimentation, implementation, and utilization of knowledge, the American educational system is fantastically productive and still the preferred model for international science and education.

QUESTION 45

Third World insecurity is growing as America seems to get weaker. We have relied on you in the past and yet you seem to be losing power. Is your power shrinking?

RESPONSE

America looks weaker in the presence of many powers. It looks weaker than it did when it was a predominant world power right after World War II. However, if you look at the number of people that are being supported, the standard of living of those people, power of industry, sophistication of communication systems, gross national product and per capita income, and the military strength at its disposal, America has never been stronger. The concentration of that power into the military sector may be comparatively less than in times past. But to say that America is losing its power and becoming weaker is really questionable; it is a comparative perception, I think.

Such observations are complicated by the fact that American power is no longer self-sufficient power. Our power is related to cooperation, interaction, and interdependance with many countries of the world, including those of Africa, Asia and Latin America. Raw materials, oil, energy sources, the need for markets and other such things are binding countries together to give them strength. America's independent, self-reliant strength has changed into an interdependent, greater strength. Still, in the perception of many people, America does not have dominant power and it seems to be getting weaker.

Today the United States is seen to be a country with less power to protect its allies and friends. It is hard to judge whether we ever really had that power, although many people thought we did have it. Clearly today, we are in a world in which there are very real limits to anybody's power: the Soviet Union's power, the United States' power, or Japan's power.

And, there are many kinds of power. How to focus power for national interest is a concern of every country. For example, the United States is, I think, increasingly aware that the developed nations have only 20% of the world population. Or, the Third World with 80% of the population consumes only 20% of the resources of the world. The developed countries enjoy the benefits from 60% to 80% of the resources of the world. That kind of imbalance is going to have to change, and there are many kinds of power that are going to leverage that change in these coming years.

When President Reagan took office, he was worried about this international perception that America was not only weaker but unwilling to use the power it did have. I believe this is why his new foreign policy was so assertive; why his commitment to substantial military budget has been so firm. He was not returning to the Cold War, but rather confirming America's strength to Americans and the world.

89

Why did the governments of Iran and Vietnam collapse? Didn't you desert them? Didn't you abandon your friends in Taiwan? Will you let other allies down? How do we look at American power today?

RESPONSE

I can remember the many criticisms of American policy in China after Mao Tse-tung gained power and Chiang Kai-shek was kicked out. One of the political cries in the United States was, "Why did we lose China? Who was responsible for our losing China?" The fact is, we never "had China." There were forces at work in China over which we neither had control nor predictable influence.

Similarly, the government of the Shah of Iran and the South Vietnamese government collapsed not because the United States withdrew its power, but because there were internal forces in those countries that produced tremendous sources of power that were hostile to those administrations.

Yes, the people we supported lost power. One way of looking at it is that they deserved to lose power because they had not maintained the support of their people. There were alternate sources of power that eventually gained control. Also, I think that we made a lot of mistakes in the years when we were not sensitive to the cultures, demands, and national interests of peoples in other countries. And, sometimes the national interests of the United States were not very well defined.

There is no doubt that American arms and American support to the Shah deeply influenced the power, developments, and circumstances in Iran during the administration of the Shah. But, like in other countries, the Shah fell because of long developed historical, personal, and politial forces within the countries over which the United States had no control. As a matter of fact, we did not have that much control over the Shah of Iran as the events of the latter period of his regime demonstrated.

Our decision concerning Taiwan was most difficult. In my opinion we did well to open relations with China, the most populous nation in the world. It was done in such a way that we would not also lose the resources, trade, and relationship with a traditional ally, Taiwan. We were taking a very important step in normalizing relationships with the Peoples Republic of China.

I think the wisdom of this decision has already been manifest as U.S./Chinese relations have turned away from the idealogical hostility and dogmatism to a more open, practical relationship. After years of Mao's rule when China was so isolated, remote and unapproachable, it is nearly miraculous to go in as I have and to see the openness, curiosity, and opportunities for positive relationships.

Taiwan is also flourishing and still under our security umbrella. It is a country that has world trade, world prestige, power, security, and prosperity for its people, even though it is not in the United Nations. And, while Taiwan was not a model of representative government in the past, there are real democratizing trends in evidence there now.

America is faithful to its allies, but now it is very difficult to exercise the same kind of overt military power that the United States could exercise right after World War II. We were the only nation that had not been devastated by the war, and we had appreciable military power. During the "cold war" period there were two dominant powers. In today's world there is no dominant power. There can be no dominant power. Even relatively small countries that were seen as powerless in the past, like Saudi Arabia and Nigeria, now have some very effective, useable power in the world community. America has not deserted its allies. But, we have not been able to control and manipulate world affairs as we could in the past. Events have taken place to change regimes in Ethiopia, Angola, Nicaragua, Vietnam, Iran, and Afghanistan. We honored our commitments to the extent of our ability. American power is still active in fighting aggression, terrorism, and disproportionate use of force, while promoting negotiation and political settlements.

QUESTION 47

Explain American actions in Vietnam, Cambodia, and Laos. Didn't you defy international law and human decency by bombing North Vietnam? Why did you intervene in a civil war in South Vietnam? Wasn't this North American neo-colonialism? Was your policy wrong? It even ruined your own economy.

RESPONSE

This very question seriously divided the American people at the time. Criticism of American actions in Vietnam was so strong that President Lyndon Johnson did not try to run for re-election, and Nixon in 1968 campaigned on the promise of getting us out of this very unpopular and destructive war.

History might be a little bit more kind in judging the United States, however, if it considers the basis of American action at that time, with the intelligence and the perspective of that time, as opposed to judging us according to the knowledge that we have now. At that time it looked like the door was closing on Asia for possibilities of open societies. It looked like communism was going to fill the vacuum created by the destruction and break-up of the political systems in Asia during World War II. The

United States became increasingly involved. And we did it poorly. We did it poorly, I say, because we went in with a great deal of ignorance about the people, their needs and desires, and the cultures of Southeast Asia. Also, consider the restraint of the American forces when time and time again we would not go over the borders into China to attack North Vietnam's supply sources. We never bombed the principal port cities because we feared that could start World War III. Many times we were criticized, as a matter of fact, for fighting the enemy with one hand tied behind our back. Moreover, we did not mobilize our domestic society or our economy; we tried to live as if we were still at peace. Of course this created horrendous inflation. We conducted a war with limited objectives; namely, to stop the encroachment of the North Vietnamese into the south with the support of the Chinese and the Soviets, and to bring a negotiated peace, "not victory."

This was not neo-colonialism. We were not seeking markets, land, or resources. We were there for a political motive, ostensibly to help a friendly, seemingly democratic government invaded by an aggressive force. In point of fact, however, the administration was not very democratic. In any event, we could not control it. The contrast between this and colonial activities of imperialist powers of the last century was great.

Many Americans will agree that this was a disastrous enterprise. The lessons learned and the sadness of this enterprise resulted in part because of American insensitivity and lack of knowledge about how to make a positive contribution to what was more than a civil war.

Vietnam became a focus of international conflict that transcended the civil war aspects of South Vietnam, Cambodia, and Laos. This was a very tragic period. For instance, the decision to bomb Cambodia was very much justified from a military point of view. Yet, because there was no formally declared war, it was seen as a breach of the peace and as an immoral act. How do you draw the line when you are fighting a war that is not declared? What is moral and what is immoral?

Today you can certainly find Americans who will argue vehemently on both sides of this particular question; feelings are mixed about what was done and how it was done in Vietnam. Americans lament what happened. It had tragic consequences for the Vietnamese, Cambodians, and Laotian peoples as seen from the sad conditions in those countries today and the fate of the refugees. It damaged our political unity, our economy, and the morale of American people. I think we are just beginning to recuperate from this situation that was filled with so many frustrations, dilemmas, and heartaches.

QUESTION 48

Are you Americans still trying to police the world even after what happened in Vietnam? Look at what you are doing in the Persian Gulf. What are you Americans doing with your power?

RESPONSE

There is a constant concern in many parts of the world about how the United States is using and will use its many powers. Such power is admittedly tremendous. Now, the United States may have learned a lesson from Vietnam. Some analysts have put it this way: America has finally seen the limits of its power in this complicated, interdependent world. I think as a nation we and our leaders, whether Republican or Democrat, realize that there truly are limits to power in today's world. We now see that every country has its own type of power. It may not be in arms, but it may certainly be in aspects of living and ruling in their own country, to say nothing of their resources and control of their people.

So I do not think that America still is trying to become a policeman of the world. The United States has some pretty well-defined concepts now. We look for diverse political systems to live and hopefully work together. We also consider our responsibility to American national interests and those of our allies. That does not mean that the United States would not use its power cooperatively if there were a challenge of aggression to the system of world commerce, trade, interaction and politics that makes possible this kind of open pluralistic society on a global basis.

If there arose a challenge to energy sources that could undermine the productivity, safety, and health of our allies in Europe and Japan, to say nothing of the United States, I think that American moral, physical, economic, and perhaps even military power could be exercised. The rapid deployment force in the Middle East is interpreted by some as being the American police force of the world when, in fact, it is more a symbolic deterrent and evidence of our will to use our power if necessary. I would like to illustrate a distinction between some of the attitudes that the United States had in the Cold War period of the 1950's and 1960's and today. We thought that through our power, persuasion, diplomacy, and the activities of the CIA, we could promote anti-Communist activities and powers as sort of a policeman of the world. We thought that we were insuring the security of others as well as ourselves. We just do not think as much in these terms anymore. To me this is a great step forward.

Experience has brought us to the understanding that we are living in an interdependent world. In an interdependent world, we cannot productively be a dominant power per se.

93

Wasn't your intervention in Chile, Israel and Iran a return to your "big stick" policies of the 1920's and before? If we have a revolution you do not approve of in our country, will you intervene again? Was Israel's attack on the PLO in Lebanon done with your agreement and support?

RESPONSE

Probably the world is in a period of re-evaluation, certainly this is true in the United States. I do not think that a "big stick" policy is possible now, partly because most countries of the world have enough protection either individually or collectively, and partly because of international public opinion. That makes it very difficult for one nation to exert its power over another. We have seen the consequences, really unexpected, of the Soviets using their "big stick" while intervening in Afghanistan in 1979. PLO terrorism and aggression provoked Israel and, in turn, Israel's use of the "big stick" has brought much criticism and some checks to its exercise of power.

I think that the possibilities of the kinds of operations in which the CIA, for example, helped the Shah overthrow the Mossadegh government are most unlikely. Not only would the American public disapprove, but such clandestine practices have been made practically impossible by the electronic communications and the accountability for actions that now exist in the international arena. We still have the exercise of force, economic as well as political, by one country or another, sometimes intentional, sometimes unintentional. However, I cannot see the return of "big stick" policies; they have not been part of American policy during these last eight or ten years.

As far as intervention, I do think that the United States will continue to help people friendly to its system or to its preferences for the international system. I think that there will be affiliation with friendly elements, even as other countries and ideologies help their friends. But I do not see any military interference; I think that the leverages of power are very different than in the "superpower" days after World War II. In today's world we have many sources of power. Many small states such as Saudi Arabia, with its oil and associated financial power, have great impact and consequence even though they are not militarily strong.

In today's interdependent world, however, I can foresee a situation in which if it looks like the productive and the financial structure of a large part of the world is going to be jeopardized by events in two or three countries, there could well be action taken, a cooperative action in that area of the world. I think this is quite different from the "big stick," although I am sure many people would argue with this. It is very hard to talk about something as complicated as this in a brief response. However, I do think that there is a clear distinction between American intervention in the affairs of other sovereign people, as in the case of "big stick" policies, and American participation in the adjudication of very important regional problems that affect large segments of the world. I do not think that American power can remain isolated from those developments either to the benefit of American national interest or to the benefit of an open, coexistent world community.

There is much debate in American about Israeli actions in Lebanon. The American government certainly knew of Israeli military preparations and growing impatience with what they considered PLO aggression from Lebanon and from terrorism. But that is much different than agreeing to and supporting the attack. Americans and the world were shocked by this violence. The work of Ambassador Habib and President Reagan to negotiate cease fire agreements and finally cessation of fighting in West Beirut showed vigorous American efforts to check Israeli use of force. The United States continues to support the United Nations resolutions and the Palestinian right to autonomy.

QUESTION 50

Do your people really support the policy of intervening in the domestic affairs of Latin American republics that your leaders consider communistic or in violation of your ideas of human rights? Don't you think that AID restrictions imposed by your Congress were an insult to these countries?

RESPONSE

In the recent history of United States relations with Latin America there have been some dramatic changes. The most visible of these changes was the negotiation of the treaty with Panama, which to some symbolized the end of colonialism in Central America. It also represented an achievement in the United States, where there were powerful political forces that felt that the Panama Canal Zone was American by right and that we should have complete control there. In recent years we have witnessed quite a change in the whole interaction process.

Now, before Watergate, the CIA did give support to those elements that were friendly and helpful to American policies in the region. Much of that activity has now stopped. Nevertheless, I do not think it is realistic to suppose that United States governmental and private attitudes are going to be less friendly to those organizations, parties, and individuals who are friendly to the United States. I just do not think that is realistic, no matter what national policy you look at.

There has been some reconsideration of American policies and interests in Latin America where President Reagan felt policies of President Carter and Congress were hurting over national interests by alienating countries like Brazil and Argentina by our restrictive policies on military assistance. It is a paradox that just as some relationships with Latin America were improving, the Falkland Island crisis intervened.

Yet, often the line between intervention and friendship is ill defined. For instance, El Salvador and other countries like Guatemala, are experiencing tragic instability. Yet, it is very difficult to know how to constructively aid the people of those countries to cut down the chances of bloodshed, turmoil, and chaos, especially when hostile outside groups are contributing to the turmoil.

In Nicaragua, Samoza had been one of those dictators that had been directly and indirectly supported by American foreign policy and actions. He lost his power partly because the United States was trying to be more even-handed and critical of those countries that did not match our perceptions of human rights and democratic development. The U.S. has since dealt with a new government in Nicaragua, despite its close contact with Cuba. An attempt has been made to work out a relationship short of intervention but which would be helpful to the development of peaceful relations between the peoples of Central American countries as well as the people of the United States and Nicaragua.

Indeed, I think that times have changed from when the United States directly intervened in these countries. However, I do not think the times have changed to where the United States government will not try to help those forces which are perceived as working for peaceful and productive solutions to our hemisphere's problems, especially if others who are hostile are intervening.

The 1982 events in the Falklands have strained many North American relations in Latin America. Many Latinos saw American opposition to the Argentine seizure of the Islands, and the subsequent assistance to NATO ally Great Britain after attempts at a negotiated settlement failed, as desertion of fellow members of the Rio Pact.

QUESTION 51

Why do you insist on our being anti-communist? Why can't you let us be friends with everyone? Why do you discourage our trade with communist countries? Isn't this just "superpower" politics?

RESPONSE

I have seen a tremendous change in American foreign policy during my career. During the early period of the Cold War, our approach to

Africa, Latin America, and many Asian countries was "stay away from those communists; they're going to subvert you; they're going to take you over in a great Communist wave. Rely on us, let us deal with them, and you stay away from them."

Today I think we are saying to many people, "Look, you need all the help you can get. If you can get it from East Germany, or West Germany, or North Korea, or South Korea, take it. But, in your own interest, do not become monopolized by any interest. Keep your options open." We do say, however, that there are political costs in dealing with the Communists, as evidenced by things happening in many countries of the world. They do have an international movement that is interested in assuming power around the world and eventually establishing a sort of commonwealth of "socialist countries."

We are not saying to people in Africa, "Don't trade with the Communists." We are saying "Do it, but take care of your national interests in dealing with them and with us."

I would answer a question like this by saying that we do not insist on any country being anti-Communist. We do suggest very strongly that they keep the doors open to all people, and that they be very careful of local groups which often cooperate with international communist movements. We hope countries are not doing things that will be harmful to the *basic* future and the development of their country and their relations with the world community (including the United States).

Still, there is no doubt that in the day-to-day operations of political, military and economic competition between our two major systems that one observes this "anti-" approach. This may be because of a very hostile competition, particularly in various countries where groups representing various ideologies are at war with each other.

On the other hand, the best "anti-" anything is a positive alternative, and I am confident that we are part of a very positive alternative to communist solutions in most countries. But we must know our competition well and be able to communicate effectively those offerings where we have alternatives for building nations, satisfying human needs, and working with the kinds of human problems that people are facing today.

A very important point for Americans to remember is that all Marxists are not hostile to United States interests and the international market system. Many socialists (Democratic Socialists, Islamic Socialists, Christian Socialists) are our friends and allies. It is many of the Marxist Leninists who promote class struggle, violent change and unyielding hostility to capitalist systems that represent the threat to peace that influences American policy.

QUESTION 52

Why do you send us such inept ambassadors who try to intervene in our country? Why do so many not know anything about our people and not speak our language?

RESPONSE

There is no question that there is great variety in the quality of ambassadors from any country. In the United States the ambassadors are appointed by the President to be his personal representatives. They are not members of the career foreign service while serving as ambassadors. Still, well over half of our ambassadors have been career diplomats who have resigned their foreign service commissions to accept a commission as the personal representative of the President. When a president leaves office, all of the ambassadors tender their resignations. The incoming president may reappoint them or accept their resignations. Career people often revert to their former status in the United States Information Agency, the Department of State, or other agencies.

Many times, for political reasons, presidents have appointed people that were active in their political campaigns, people who contributed to their success in gaining the presidency. Because each one of these ambassadors must be confirmed by the Senate, it has become more and more difficult for controversial or incompetent persons to get an ambassadorship since they must face the examination of both the Senate and the inquisitive, powerful media.

That does not mean that you will always get someone who speaks the language fluently. I will give you a good example. The ambassador that Mr. Carter appointed to Saudi Arabia did not speak Arabic. He had been the governor of the state of South Carolina and a very close affiliate and supporter of President Carter during his campaign in 1976. I think that Ambassador West was an effective ambassador, mainly because the Saudis valued having an ambassador who enjoyed a personal, confidential relationship with the President of the United States. He was able to get Mr. Carter to visit Saudi Arabia on one of his first foreign trips. Ambassador West did have a staff that knew the language well and that had the knowledge to back him up. So the ambassador himself does not necessarily have to be an expert in the language, the country, or the culture.

Competent ambassadors are usually successful people, either in government or outside of government. Once they get the responsibility, the great majority of them work very hard to become acquainted with that country's culture, politics, and leadership so they can do a reputable job representing their country assisted by their "country-teams", who are mostly career foreign service officers representing the various federal organizations active in foreign affairs.

So it is a mixed bag; there is no doubt about it. But I think that the "disaster" ambassadors that we have had in the past have become fewer in number. With their increased visibility, more accountability has been expected. The Senate also has been increasingly demanding before confirming any ambassador. Standards are much higher than they were in the past.

With reference to the question of intervening in other countries, it has become much less frequent for an American ambassador to be so accused or charged. It is much more difficult for an ambassador to be a power broker now, even if he or she so desired. With worldwide instantaneous communications, the senior officials in Washington often manage any crises, thereby reducing the power of the ambassador.

I think we have to be forthright about another thing. The ambassador's job is to promote America's national interest. In his advocacy and promotion of American interests, people who are critical are going to say that this is intervention. There is a fine line here; the nature of any action is often in the eye of the beholder.

In some countries, such as the Philippines, the American Embassy is very large. Many organizations are represented there. For example, the Veteran's Administration, the FBI, the Library of Congress, the Department of Labor, the Department of Commerce, and the Department of Agriculture all have envoys. All of these organizations have personnel that are active in working in specific programs of interest both to the people of the Philippines and to the United States. The magnitude of this activity, in addition to the assistance programs and the military programs, is often interpreted as intervention by critics.

QUESTION 53
Why don't you give all of the Panama Canal back to Panama now?
RESPONSE

I remember Ambassador Ellsworth Bunker, our great senior diplomat, and his painful negotiating of treaties of mutual security. Recognizing the sovereignty of the Republic of Panama over the Panama Canal, he worked out a meaningful arrangement. It provided for the economic and the security interests of not only Panama, but of the nations participating in the Organization of American States. They all have a very vital part in the economic, political, and security interests involved in the functioning and the availability of the Panama Canal.

One of the achievements of the Carter administration was to finally bring that treaty into being and to start the process of bringing the Panamanians into control and management of the canal. There has been a gradual training, a gradual handover, a gradual rearrangement of many of the things in the operation of the canal and of the military installations that the United States has had there for hemispheric security. A very orderly process of transition has been negotiated and accepted by the Panamanian and American people in their mutual interest.

Incidently, the treaty triggered a great debate in our own Congress, as well as in different political groupings in Panama. Still, I think that in this particular case we have very successfully disarmed the charge that the United States was holding the only remaining colony in the world, the Panama Canal. We do not hold it. If you go down and see the changes taking place and what kinds of people are handling the money, resources, and power in the canal zone, you will see that the charge of neo-colonialism vis-a-vis Panama is not an accurate portrayal of what is happening. There has been a real change.

QUESTION 54

What is the Peace Corps? Are they really CIA agents, or are they just young people who can't get jobs?
RESPONSE

The U.S. Peace Corps is operating in about 60 countries by invitation from those countries. There are some 5000 volunteers around the world. I have worked with the Peace Corps, and I have a great respect for them. I am deeply grateful to the countries that have hosted Peace Corps projects because it has been a fantastic education for thousands of young and old Americans who have served in this capacity.

Peace Corps volunteers are a mixed bag. In the early days, they were mostly young, idealistic liberal arts generalists, or college educated people looking for an opportunity to represent their country in a humane way; to make a contribution to peace, national development, world development, and friendship. During the Vietnam war period, we began to see a change in volunteers. Sometimes they were just young people who had decided to avoid the draft and military service. But more importantly, standards for selecting volunteers changed. Soon most of the countries said, "Don't send us these generalists. We need people with specific skills to help our people in specific areas," So the recruiting for the Peace Corps began to concentrate more on specific skills that leaders in the countries felt they needed. Often, that meant bringing in middle-aged people, sometimes elderly people. One of those elderly people was President Carter's mother who went to India.

These people definitely are not CIA agents; they are volunteer Americans. The Peace Corps volunteers are actually quite a contrast to our foreign service or civil service people who are working overseas. They are sort of quasi-government; they are not careerists; they are not under the pension system nor the career discipline system of the federal government.

These young people have joined for a great variety of purposes. Some of them were not able to get jobs. Many have had jobs and careers but wanted to add an international dimension to their lives. Many have a conviction, perhaps a religious conviction, that they want to make a contribution in a developing country. Some of them are just trying to escape a personal situation where they might have to marry someone if they do not get out of town. There is a tremendous variety of motivation. Still, I would give the Peace Corps a "B " in my own personal evaluation for their effort, for their ideal, and for the concept; maybe a "C-" for actual achievement. Although some of them have done remarkable things, they usually make a very limited contribution in the 18 months or two years that they are overseas. Most returned volunteers readily grant that they learn more than they actually contribute to developing societies or institutions. The Peace Corps continues its vital activity because it benefits the country served on their terms and it benefits the volunteers who are serving.

QUESTION 55

Why has the United States been picking on some of its friends over the human rights issue? Don't you realize that strong measures are needed to protect society against attacks by terrorist groups? Look at how you sabotaged your friends in Iran.

RESPONSE

This has been a very pointed question from countries like Uruguay, Brazil, Argentina, and Chile where governments have been locked in fights with local terrorist and opposition forces that have been trying to overthrow them. Some say we are being unrealistic, that we do not practice what we preach on civil rights even in our own country, and that if our national interests seem to dictate it, we will support other countries that have worse records than they do. They feel that they have an excuse because they are fighting terrorism in the way they feel they have to fight it to maintain their regimes as well as to maintain their position of being able to be a friend of the United States.

This is a dilemma confronting American foreign policy and its origin does not rest merely on the whims of a specific administration. Members of Congress had written laws requiring the monitoring of human rights concerns even before Carter became President. These actions have tended to put pressure on people responsible for carrying out American foreign policy to take note of actions that fall short of basic standards of human rights that have been articulated by the United Nations and that have been accepted by most nations.

The international results of this have been mixed; sometimes the effect has been to withhold support to the friendly countries that are faced with difficult security problems. On the other hand there are indications that these policies have brought increased justice, and the review and reduction of political torture and persecution in many cases.

Of course, debate will continue about whether or not the United States withdrew support from the Shah of Iran, giving him conflicting signals. There is equal criticism, not only from many Iranian patriots but also from many Americans, claiming we should have tried to force the Shah to be much more democratic much earlier in his administration.

The fact is that the human rights problem probably takes on a different style of implementation for every government and people. Essential aspects of American foreign policy and national purpose are to promote individual freedom, the rule of law, governments and exercises of power that guard against inhumane treatment, torture, unfair seizure of property, and the breach of basic legal norms.

In the United States, of course, we tend to conduct our programs in accordance with the ideals that we see in our own law. Many times we are not practicing what we preach; every country has a gap between the realities of their lives and their aspirations and ideals. One of the functions of American society, as we have seen it, is to hold up worthy ideals and worthy goals, even though we and our friends often fall short of them. Again, this is a policy that is being seriously examined by the new administration in Washington. It will be interesting to see what adjustments are made, both in style and in content, coming both from the Executive branch and from the American Congress.

We also need to remember that many times today's terrorists and heroes in liberation movements or in political revolutions are tomorrow's national leaders. We see an example of this in Begin, the prime minister of Israel, who was a terrorist against the British and a terrorist in fighting the Arab interests that challenged the early days of Israel's existence. There are many examples, whether it be Nicaragua or other places, where people who are terrorists come to power, and once they have the mantle of responsibility of national leadership, they are no longer antilaw.

We have seen this in communist revolutions; when the communists are given power, they function much differently than when they are seeking power. They break every conceivable law in the fight for power, but once they get in they become extremely conservative, extremely intolerant of differences, and unforgiving of any breaking of laws that they establish. So we have to be careful of our words here. It is very difficult to judge whether a country is using its police power to maintain stability and avoid chaos in a responsible way, or whether it is a group of people in a dictatorial, unaccountable exercise of power, be it fascist, communist or any other kind of authoritarian rule. Again, this is one of the constant dilemmas for formulators of American policy because in today's world we often have a coalition of "good" guys and another of "bad" guys. It is difficult to separate them and to define American national interests in maximizing the relations that would be most helpful for developing a peaceful world and meaningful relations between countries. These are rough, demanding questions because they concern dynamic, changing situations throughout the world.

QUESTION 56

Many people say your position on human rights is hypocritical since you still discriminate against blacks and other minorities. How do you justify passing judgment on other countries?

RESPONSE

Often people really believe something and would like to practice it. However, as life unfolds they are not able to practice it, either because of the complexity of their own personal lives, or the situation at the time.

The "Wilmington 10" incident involving blacks convicted of crimes in the South was well covered in our courts and in our press. Some remedial measures have been taken to recognize some of the injustices suffered in the legal proceedings in that case in North Carolina.

As for the riots in Miami, the black community was resentful of the fact that their community was not, in their eyes, getting fair opportunities for education and for other services in the community. On top of that, in came thousands of Cuban refugees who often received governmental, state, federal, and private support to help them get located, obtain jobs, educate their children, and in general receiving help the American blacks could not get.

All of this was then complicated by an event which the black community saw as a miscarriage of justice. In the process of an arrest, a black citizen of Miami was brutalized and killed by the police. The police had not been disciplined or convicted for the act. That event finally sparked a series of riots that brought to the surface black feelings of discrimination and hopelessness.

These are things that are most regrettable. But, it does not mean that you do not have laws, rules, and principles of how the society should work with justice and with opportunity for all. Likewise, we should have human rights criteria in connection with our international activities. We support these criteria in the United Nations. We support them as much as we can in our individual dealings and in our criticism of our own activities. Just because we have problems in the United States that are unresolved does not mean that we should not have ideals and high standards, particularly if we can do a better job of meeting them in the future.

QUESTION 57

How can the U.S. explain the inconsistency of its policy in denying arms credit to Uruguay and Argentina because of human rights violations while making vast shipments of arms to the Middle East, Korea, and elsewhere?

RESPONSE

There are many apparent inconsistencies in the policies of the United States. Our policies are so complicated and wide ranging that they touch almost every country of the world. When you look at the interests of the United States as reflected in American foreign policy, made both by the Executive branch and Congress, these seeming inconsistencies are particularly evident in crisis areas.

For example, there is a part of our policy that touches on relations with the Soviet Union, the only nation viewed as having the potential of radically damaging our national interests. Russia has a record of activities that seem to be hostile and threatening to the interests not only of the United States but also of our allies. When you get into one part of the world, such as North Asia (Korea and Japan), Afghanistan, or Iran, you will find that the United States, in setting its priorities, will take into consideration the dimension of Soviet involvement and threat as it is perceived by American policymakers.

On the other hand, with countries that are far removed from the Soviet Union, such as those in South America, there is a different set of priorities. It would certainly support the validity of our policies if we could be consistent and even-handed on human rights requirements. But, there are different kinds of problems in different parts of the world. These differences do affect the priorities and do create inconsistencies, particularly in the eyes of those people who are critical or who are directly affected by such inconsistencies.

104

Will this Egyptian-Israeli Treaty work? In helping to set it up, didn't you abandon other allies in the Middle East, like the Saudis? They opposed this treaty. Also, you are not adequately considering the Palestinians.

RESPONSE

Dealing with Arab-Israeli relations, but more specifically with the Egyptian-Israeli Treaty, is one of the most difficult questions faced by Americans. I have heard many variants of this complex question, each reminding me of the earlier frustrations of many of us working in Middle Eastern affairs. Then we confronted the seeming impossibility of ever getting Israelis and Arabs, or Egyptians, to even sit down at the same negotiating table.

Yet with the passage of time, with the Camp David Accords as the treaty is called, the two most powerful nations involved in the Middle East crisis not only sat down and negotiated, but also took some substantial steps toward peace. They even have opened their borders to trade and tourism. In addition, land taken from the Egyptians, including oil resources, have been returned. Some groundwork has been laid for the negotiation of crucial and agonizing problems dealing with the rights and the interests of the Palestinians as well as the interrelations of all the Arab countries.

As we have seen recently the Arab countries of the Middle East do enjoy general concensus; yet they have no essential cooperation among themselves. With the Iranian-Iraqi war the Syrians broke off their relationship with the Iraqis, and the Libyans also have backed the Iranians and not the Arabic Iraqis. This tremendously confusing situation makes bringing together these once antagonistic nations, on a step by step basis, to where they are willing and able to negotiate, almost miraculous. They can make some meaningful steps towards reducing hostility, reducing the danger of overt warfare, and beginning a process of negotiation, treaty-making, and the carrying out of specific acts that could build some kind of hope for a settlement.

Now the Soviets, of course, in the meetings in Geneva, were pushing as we were for a comprehensive treaty. When we began to work out the details, we found it was impossible to get agreement among all of the vested interests involved. The stalemate and the lack of activity created the situation in which one man, in a very heroic step, broke the stalemate. President Sadat made the unprecedented departure of going to Jerusalem and beginning the process that made the Camp David negotiations possible.

We have shown through our continued support to the United Nations and through contributions to many charitable international organizations, that help from the United States is available to the people of the Middle East and to the Palestinians, who are actually spread throughout the Middle East in many countries. We acknowledge their right to exist. We have acknowledged that the security considerations for the survival of Israel, on the part of the Israelis and of the United States, have made it very difficult to meet some of the demands and ambitions of the Palestinians and their descendants. In the Camp David Accords there is a provision that negotiation should begin, and it has begun, to end the Israeli occupation of the so called "West Bank," and to take specific steps over a period of years to bring rights, sovereignty, justice and security to the Palestinians in that part of the world.

How that can be done, be it by creating an independent Palestinian nation, or their becoming part of Jordan, or becoming a semi-autonomous state with some responsibility to Israel and some responsibility to Jordan, or through providing some self-rule by the Palestinians themselves. These are things still to be negotiated. But I think that the Egyptian-Israeli treaty was a "miracle," breaking an unbelievable, irrational log-jam. It has taken some very solid steps that perhaps not only have delayed war, but also have made it possible for people to interact and to communicate in a way that was absolutely impossible only four or five years ago.

We might also add that the oil issue is a very important factor. Large segments of the American public have become aware of the actions of President Sadat and his successor. Also there is an expanded awareness of Arabic interests because of our national dependence on Middle Eastern oil. Arabic interests, for the first time over the last five years, have had enough resources to be able to compete in the field of public relations. They have been able to project and communicate their side of the Arab-Israeli issue to the American public. We are beginning to see that many Americans are not so sure that the Egyptian-Israeli Treaty is a good thing, particularly for those Arabs who have roots in Arabic countries that are against the treaty.

This is still a very fluid situation. I think that American policy will continue to be absolutely firm on guaranteeing the security and survival of Israel. On the other hand, blind defense of the Israelis in whatever they do is gone forever as seen in the American reaction to the Israeli move into Lebanon. These last years have educated the American people and especially the American leaders about the importance and legitimacy of Arabic interests, as well as teaching us how to promote American national interests in this part of the world.

Diplomacy is an art. Considerable time, energy, and effort are going into assuring much better quality negotiations than in the past. We were sort of one-sided, taking that part of the world for granted and literally putting the Middle East on the "back burner" during the period of Vietnam and during the period of the Cold War when the Soviet Union was the focus, not the Middle East. Now, the Middle East is a prime focus, and it is getting some of the energy and quality attention it deserves.

QUESTION 59

Why have you pressured and isolated Cuba? They could not hurt you! You have even reconciled with China.

RESPONSE

This special case exists just ninety miles from the United States. Unfortunately, it is not just something between the Cuban and American people. Cubans have been caught in a competition between two systems with competing ideologies.

Castro and the communists in South America, with in recent intrusions in Africa and some parts of Asia, have been extremely active in fighting the system they say they are against, namely, imperialism, capitalism, and colonialism in any form. Still, Carter tried to achieve reconciliation. But, every time we would get on the brink of a reconciliation, Cuba would intervene in Angola, Ethiopia, or somewhere in Africa or South America. Hostilities were rekindled.

We have also been concerned with the Soviet influence in Cuba. There, as in other areas where the Soviet Union has intervened, we have seen a subversion of interests that we feel are important for building a peaceful and pluralistic world society, to say nothing of the threat of Soviet supplied armaments in Cuba.

Although we have not yet been able to reconcile with Castro, many people in the American government have tried to promote the normalization process. Then, just when we get close to a breakthrough, we have something happen, like when Castro permitted a very large number of people that were causing him trouble to flee Cuba. These "boat people" alleviated some of his internal domestic strife. These kinds of events have brought a disruption of any possible negotiations. They have happened repeatedly.

Most Americans probably would like to re-establish normal relations with Cuba. And, there was a beginning of "normalization." As a matter of fact, Castro allowed thousands of Cuban-Americans who had come to the United States and who had made their lives quite prosperous to go back to Cuba as tourists. This unleashed some very real problems for him, because it gave the people of Cuba ideas they did not have before. This partly stimulated the great migration of the "boat people," with over a hundred thousand Cubans coming out of Cuba because they wanted to try another way of life.

QUESTION 60
You are supposed to be leaders of the democratic world. Why do you support dictatorships and military juntas?
RESPONSE

We have a very interesting dilemma here. We have distinguished between our approach towards Communist dictatorships and non-Communist dictatorships. We generally have been put in a position of opposition to Communist dictatorships because they have been affiliated with a world movement that challenges the American system and American national interests. We have been less willing to openly challenge countries like Nicaragua and Chile which have forms of control much different from what we would like to see. We cannot intervene and be the policemen in every part of the world, however. This prompts us to be most concerned with the practices of actual or potential enemies.

I think that Spain is a good example of another aspect of this dilemma. For years we did not recognize Francisco Franco because he was a fascist. Many groups in the U.S. had supported the republican forces during the Spanish Civil War, and they were able to keep American legislators and diplomats from recognizing Franco. Now, did Franco fall because we did not recognize him? No. Actually, he was able to be even more dictatorial because there were no outside influences from the United States, or from any other countries coming in to educate the people, to give them alternatives and hope. He was able to draw the cloak of isolation around him and to be even more dictatorial than he was before.

After Spain began to open up, after we recognized Spain, and after we began to have trade, interaction, cooperative arrangements and military bases there, fascism began to be seriously undermined. People began to have mobility, dignity, alternatives, and contact with other than fascist countries.

This has been a very difficult problem through the years because there are special interest groups in the United States that have tended to support certain groups that were not democratic. On the other hand certain groups have vigorously opposed that position. We have had these fights in Congress and other places, trying to wrestle with this basic problem: how much does the United States intervene in the affairs of another country, and do we deny recognition of a government and normal relations with the people just because we do not approve of their government?

This is a very tough question. Sometimes, I think, we have answered it well, keeping contacts open and helping people move to a higher standard of living and freedom. In other cases, I am afraid that we have supported certain authoritarian governments with the net effect of thwarting basic possibilities and developments in those countries. I think history is currently teaching us many valuable lessons as the results of some of our past policies have become clear.

Epilogue

This epilogue is to further assist those who wish to become better prepared as citizen ambassadors for answering questions about the United States.

1. Why do people around the world ask questions about America?

There are several reasons why non-Americans ask Americans questions about the United States. Many have real concerns about issues, policies, and future actions of Americans, governments, and other influential organizations. Some may be only curious.

Others may have anti-American tendencies and resentments which have been brought to their minds by observing other Americans or reading propaganda (local or international). The media (television, films, and print) has also had a significant impact.

Sometimes, non-Americans ask hard, critical questions because they have been asked similar questions by people in their own country. They may feel a need to find appropriate responses for others as well as themselves.

2. What types of questions do foreigners ask Americans?

Many initial questions may not be only for information. Questions may be probing attitudes, attention, interest, or status. People may be asking, in effect, "How is this American going to treat me?"

Questions asked by non-Americans are often about generally held stereotypes. Quite sharp questions may be posed without meaning to offend or confuse. If the questioner does not use English fluently, the language expressed may not always convey the subtleties of the originator's thoughts, and queries may come across bluntly, if not offensively.

Some people obviously ask belligerent questions with the purpose of being critical. However, people may also ask sincere yet critical questions. There are times when people are interested, but their way of asking questions may appear awkward. Those who respond should usually suspend judgment and not misinterpret intent.

3. Which Americans are most often asked potentially difficult questions by non-Americans?

People in powerful governmental positions, such as embassy officers, are asked many tough questions. Military service personnel, Peace Corps volunteers and missionaries are also often asked searching questions. However, if they make a mistake in answering, it usually is not as noticable as if a U.S. government official makes a quotable blunder. Foreign presses seem to enjoy "official blunders" as much as the American press.

It is safe to assume that any American (tourist, businessman, and visiting professor or student) is a contestant for a non-American to play the questioning game with. For some reason, all Americans are expected to be knowledgeable about themselves and their systems.

4. How do you respond to questions that non-Americans might ask you because you are an American?

Although answering questions is always a personal matter, with individual style, there are some useful basic guidelines which might be followed to help make an encounter positive.

Take each question as if it were sincere! If the queries are hostile or critical and you respond facetiously or with a sarcastic or negative "put down," you automatically cut off the channel of desirable communication. In conversation, people often mirror your attitude. If you respond haughtily they may reciprocate. If you are suspicious, they will probably be suspicious. If you are friendly (open), even if somewhat reserved, they will most likely act friendly towards you even if there is not agreement on an issue. Be careful not to misinterpret the tone or style of questioners.

People who speak English as a second language do not always have the ability to use non-verbal expressions which give real meaning to inquiries. Be careful to "read between the lines" for what is truly wanted, even if it seems stilted or unsure.

If you are asked a question and do not have the facts or sufficient experience to respond well, the very least you should say is that you are not an expert on the subject. Tell them that you hope they will understand your limited experience about a particular question. Try to draw out their concerns and build rapport with them. By all means, do not say either directly or indirectly that you are not going to answer a question because you have been instructed not to! Say instead that you are responding from a limited perspective, but that you are genuinely interested in the questioner's feelings.

Aside from giving your opinion, it is also important to give factual information to the questioner. If you do not have reliable information, you could say that you do not know much about it, but that you may be willing to get better information if it is considered essential.

Repeatedly saying, "I don't know", or somehow expressing rejection may be the worst response. For example, you do not want to say, "I did not come here to talk about that!" or "I do not want to 'rock the boat' or say something that might be offensive." Saying that you do not discuss certain subjects or that you do not want to or cannot answer a certain question that may be important to the person can cause the non-American to wonder if you have anything important to share with them at all. You may be considered rude.

Here are some possible approaches to responding to such questions. (These are not definite "answers," only tentative responses.) If you are frustrated by the question and unable to give some kind of response, these prefaces might work:

"My own impression is that ... "
"My experience has been ... "
"This is how I feel at this time: ... "

Keep in mind that many of the non-American questions are not only for information. They are sometimes "games." The questioner may already have a fixed opinion and just wants to see how you might react. They may not be as interested in listening to the content of *what* you say as in *how* you respond, or *why!*

5. Where can you go to find responses which can be appropriate for particularly hard questions?

Try brief official statements from the U.S. State Department which might help in answering some of the more specific questions about U.S. policies. Americans going abroad can write to the State Department Office of Publications for speeches, summary statements, and basic restatements and background facts on countries and peoples.

If you have regular occasion to be an "unofficial representative of America" you might want to have your state Senator(s) put you on a mailing list for information updates. Other country embassy mailing lists could include you. Addresses are available through major libraries or your local Congressman.

There is a problem in this method of gathering useful information, however. Most people, if they will tell you honestly, are not interested in political statements or lengthy reports. Most would appreciate a concise response, one that is "ready to use."

Those who are near major universities can inquire of professors, or even take some classes dealing with such "answers" to most often asked questions. Study groups and embassy attachés are other sources of simple responses. Remember to get a variety of responses, because both situations and needs will vary for *you*. There are no "pat answers" that will suffice all questioners and questions. Practice can help you determine differing approaches to use.

It is also strongly recommended that you take pictures in the host country when you first arrive. Look for situations and "things" that are similar to home, and those that are different (eating places, means of transportation, methods of communicating, etc.). If you record your reactions to each of the pictures, then at a later time reevaluate your ideas, you will usually come up with new vistas of what people locally have on their mind, as you find your own reactions changing or finding a new focus.

6. Why is it that some people do not ask questions of Americans?

People from other cultures are often embarrassed to seek out necessary information. Sometimes they are over-awed by an "outsider." They may feel that asking questions is inappropriate, or they may be inhibited by expectations of courtesy or lack of perspective on their part. Few of us want to ask "dumb questions." Responses which might be helpful do not seem worth "losing face."

Some people have not learned *how* to ask or *what* to question. Others have learned *not* to ask questions. For example, many Asians will not often directly pose problems. As a cultural courtesy, it is felt more appropriate to "skirt the issue" and let it appear naturally. Nor would many people express personal feelings to others, especially "foreigners." Of course, this is not to say that people are not naturally inquisitive or that they avoid questions. What is implied is that directly confronting those outside their own culture seems undesirable even if information or understanding is needed.

7. If non-Americans do not normally ask Americans questions, how does the American get them to inquire about what may be useful and appropriate?

If there is some hesitancy in posing legitimate inquiries, there are "general openers" which might be effective in bringing up what might be wanted. The American might comment, for example, that something about the host's country has been said, with a request for information as to its correctness. This may show the non-American that the American is trying to understand a country and its people. It also gives the potential questioner something to express agreement or disagreement about in the spirit of helpfulness.

Naturally, there are countries and cultures where either sex or age may preclude the willingness to respond with an opinion. Status also may be inhibiting. An employee might not want to be put on a par with a foreign employer. More indirect approaches requiring a simple yes/no response could be most useful, particularly in groups.

The American might also say that he or she was talking to someone and was told something about which the facts are still unclear. One might say, "In my experience, this is not familiar to me. Please help me to understand how it is here." This could generate other questions and lead to what is desirable to ask or be asked about.

Another opener might be to ask people in the host country how they feel about what Americans have done in controversial situations that could be embarrassing, such as Watergate, Vietnam, El Salvador or disarmament. Such openers show the potential questioners in the host country that the American will not be embarrassed about talking openly with other people about the United States. It shows that the American is willing to share ideas. This helps the non-American ask questions within the context of propriety, friendship, and hospitality. It can be refreshing to see that the American is not trying to deceive the hosts, freeing them to more easily express their concerns.

8. How can returning Americans help others getting ready for a similar overseas experience?

Returning Americans can be asked what two or three questions (or examples of erroneous stereotype behavior or conditions) they had when in host countries. They can often think of what seemed to surprise them upon arriving, or conditions which were of apparent interest to people they met.

Americans usually return home with insightful answers to such questions as "What makes Americans so wasteful? Why do they use such big cars and waste gas needed in other countries? Why do they spend so much time and money on material things? Why is the tempo of life so hurried?"

Questions about American policy abroad and about American actions and programs in other countries often come to the surface while Americans visit abroad. Critical queries are sometimes posed. Returning Americans may have helpful responses to questions such as, "Why does your own government help our local dishonest or corrupt officials?" Or, "Couldn't more of American foreign aid be more useful here than in buying armaments for our neighbors to use against us?"

Helpful suggestions from returning Americans to those preparing to travel or live overseas have been to keep an open mind and avoid hasty judgments. Fixed ideas are often not too valid even after visiting with a variety of people. People in any country or culture are as different as in one's own.

9. What else can returning Americans do to help build bridges of understanding between Americans and others throughout the world?

Americans can initiate conversation with other people about what seems important to them and those with whom they have been in contact. Many do not share their feelings about their overseas experience unless they are talking with someone who has been to the country visited, or unless someone asks them about their experiences directly.

There also should be some way to recognize and show appreciation to returning Americans, so that they will exert themselves and keep open their contacts and friendships which were made abroad. Returning Americans may want to become acquainted with people in the embassies and consulates in America for the countries they have visited.

It can be helpful to visit with friends, employers, and associates, and to share ideas and questions. If people think, "That takes too much time and energy, and I may never go back to that country anyway, so why should I?", they lose out and so do others who travel where they have been.

What else? In reviewing some of the reasons for both seeking and responding to questions, each American has an opportunity to better understand what being American can mean, not only for others, but for one's self. Obviously, many other reasons for studying possible circumstances that tend to provoke misunderstanding could be reviewed.

What seems important in this exercise is that bridges of understanding can be built for those who want to know, to feel, and to be positive about what being and living "American" entails.